HEF

Also by Frank Topping

All the Days of My Life
Grappling with God
An Impossible God
Laughing In My Sleep

Here I Stand

A Collection of Passions and Convictions

Edited by Frank Topping

Hodder & Stoughton
LONDON SYDNEY AUCKLAND

British Library Cataloguing in Publication Data
A record for this book is available from the British Library

ISBN 0 340 74539 8

Typeset by Avon Dataset Ltd, Bidford-on-Avon, Warks

Printed and bound in Great Britain by
Mackays of Chatham PLC, Chatham, Kent

Hodder and Stoughton
A division of Hodder Headline PLC
338 Euston Road
London NW1 3BH

To
Anne and Robert, Simon and Jane, Mark and Rachel,
whose encouragement, wit and warmth
has enriched my life considerably

Here I stand; I can do no other.
God help me. Amen!

Martin Luther (1483–1546)

Speech at the Diet of Worms, 18 April 1521

Contents

Acknowledgments

Every effort has been made to trace sources and to seek permission from the owners of copyright material. In cases where this has not been possible, we apologise and will do all that we can to rectify the situation in subsequent editions.

We gratefully acknowledge the following that appear in this book: an extract from *Gridlock* by Ben Elton (1991), published by Little Brown & Company and reprinted by permission; an extract from *Autogeddon* by Heathcote Williams (Jonathan Cape, 1991); an extract from the Revd Dr Martin Luther King Jnr's speech 'I Have a Dream' (copyright 1963 by Martin Luther King Jr., copyright renewed 1991 by Coretta Scott King), reprinted by arrangement with The Heirs to the Estate of Martin Luther King, Jr., c/o Writers House, Inc. as agent for the proprietor; an extract from *Treat Me Right* by Ian Kennedy (1988), © Ian Kennedy 1988 and reprinted by permission of Oxford University Press; an extract from *Moral Dilemmas in Medicine* by Alistair V. Campbell (Churchill Livingstone), reprinted by permission; an article by Melanie Phillips in *The Observer* (19 May 1997), © The Observer and reprinted by permission; an extract from Winston Churchill's BBC broadcast of 18 June 1940, reprinted by permission of HMSO; an article by Colin Tudge in the *Independent on Sunday* (16 March 1997), reprinted by permission; 'Do not go gentle into that good night' by Dylan Thomas, taken from *The Dylan Thomas Omnibus* (Phoenix, 1995), reprinted by permission of David Higham Associates; a leader from the *Independent* (29 October 1996), reprinted by permission; an article by Paul Barker in *The Guardian* (4 November 1996), © The Guardian and reprinted by permission; an extract from 'Notes on the Art of Poetry' by Dylan Thomas, reprinted by permission of David Higham Associates; two extracts from *Liberating Sex* by Adrian Thatcher (SPCK, 1993), reprinted by permission of SPCK; an article by Suzanne Moore in *The Independent* (7 February 1997), reprinted by permission; an article by Andrew Brown in *The Independent* (Good Friday, 1997), reprinted by permission.

Introduction

'Here I stand; I can do no other.' Martin Luther's defiant declaration, which arguably brought about the most profound religious and cultural reformation of this millennium, sums up for me both the passion and the commitment to reason, logic and intelligence of the thinker and advocate. 'Passion' is certainly a key word in this anthology, but then so are 'reason', 'logic' and 'intelligence'.

Some writers can spend days honing a particular sentence, re-phrasing it, searching for the right word, but there are also times when the same person cannot write fast enough, when words tumble out, cascading onto the page, when the writer is driven by a merciless, inner daemon. Sometimes the truth or the essence of the matter pursued seems elusive and all that can be achieved is an awareness of an unseen goal, tantalisingly beyond the horizon being searched; at other times conviction comes with such startling clarity it is as if the words were leaping into the writer's mind or mouth, demanding declaration.

Conviction, prejudice, truth and error can all be arrived at through the process of slow and laborious effort or they can come in the white heat of passion. However they are reached, and however much we agree or disagree, most of us are endlessly fascinated by other people's opinions, convictions and dilemmas.

There is breathtaking drama in the torrent of anger and abuse that poured from the mouth of Oliver Cromwell as he summarily dismissed the 'Rump' parliament. There is poetry in the phrasing of Martin Luther King's great speech, 'I have a dream' which belongs, of course, to a completely different age and style from that of the pedantic 'i' dotting and 't' crossing exactitude of the Athanasian Creed; and what tragic irony there is in the speech of the great

1

philosopher, Socrates, as he argues for his life in the face of prejudice and bigotry.

Abortion, war, euthanasia, marriage, death, evil, birth, original sin, God, faith, religion, creativity, inspiration, science ... any anthology put together by an individual, and this individual in particular, will be by its very nature prejudiced and limited. Prejudiced in that there has been no attempt to strike a politically correct balance of arguments, and prejudiced in that there are some opinions and arguments I find so vile and repulsive that I simply do not wish to give them houseroom; and limited, well, by the enormity of my ignorance and by the economy of pages available for this first edition.

Already I hear the cry, 'But there is absolutely no mention of . . .'

Yes, I know, I know. There are subjects I barely touch on, or even fail to represent, which deserve an anthology of their own, and there are subjects which are of little interest to some readers but which have fascinated me beyond measure and have been given an inordinate amount of space. That, I think, is the nature of an anthology, as opposed to a dictionary. I dare to hope that this book might be the beginning of a collection of views, convictions and opinions that will grow in future editions, with contributions pouring in from every direction, who knows. However, I believe there is a sufficient variety and quantity of ideas and points of view expressed here to keep most households, common rooms or indeed sixth forms in goodly debate for some considerable time. Enjoy!

Frank Topping
Thornbury, 1997

Part 1 Ethical Issues

1. Abolition of Slavery

William Wilberforce was one of the three founder members of the anti-slavery society formed in Britain in 1787. He was the MP for Hull and a close friend of William Pitt the Younger. In 1788 Wilberforce fell seriously ill. He obtained a promise from Pitt, by that time Prime Minister, that he would try to abolish the slave trade, and Pitt became as committed to ending the slave trade as Wilberforce. By 1789 Wilberforce recovered and was able to continue his battle. In Parliament, on 12 May 1789, he made this powerful speech against the trade in African slaves.

When we consider the vastness of the continent of Africa; when we reflect how all other countries have for some centuries past been advancing in happiness and civilization; when we think how in this same period all improvement in Africa has been defeated by her intercourse with Britain; when we reflect that it is we ourselves that have degraded them to that wretched brutishness and barbarity which we now plead as the justification of our guilt; how the slave trade has enslaved their minds, blackened their character, and sunk them so low in the scale of animal beings that some think the apes are of a higher class, and fancy the orang-outang has given them the go-by. What a mortification must we feel at having so long neglected to think of our guilt, or attempt any reparation! It seems, indeed, as if we had determined to forbear from all interference until the measure of our folly and wickedness was so full and complete; until the impolicy which eventually belongs to vice was become so plain and glaring that not an individual in the country should refuse to join in the abolition; it seems as if we had waited until the persons most interested should be tired out with the folly and nefariousness of the trade, and should unite in petitioning against it.

Let us then make such amends as we can for the mischiefs we have done to the unhappy Continent; let us recollect what Europe itself was no longer ago than three or four centuries. What if I should be able to show this House that in a civilized part of Europe, in the time of our Henry VII, there were people who actually sold their own children? What if I should tell them that England itself was that country? What if I should point out to them that the very place where this inhuman traffic was carried on was the City of Bristol? Ireland at that time used to drive a considerable trade in slaves with these neighbouring barbarians; but a great plague having infested the country, the Irish were struck with a panic, suspected (I am sure very properly) that the plague was a punishment sent from heaven for the sin of the slave trade, and therefore abolished it. All I ask, therefore, of the people of Bristol is, that they would become as civilized now as Irishmen were four hundred years ago. Let us put an end at once to this inhuman traffic – let us stop this effusion of human blood. The true way to virtue is by withdrawing from temptation; let us then withdraw from these wretched Africans, those temptations to fraud, violence, cruelty, and injustice, which the slave trade furnishes. Wherever the sun shines, let us go round the world with him, diffusing our beneficence; but let us not traffic, only that we may set kings against their subjects, subjects against their kings, sowing discord in every village, fear and terror in every family, setting millions of our fellow-creatures a-hunting each other for slaves, creating fairs and markets for human flesh through one whole continent of the world, and, under the name of policy, concealing from ourselves all the baseness and iniquity of such a traffic.

Why may we not hope, ere long, to see Hanse-towns established on the coast of Africa as they were on the Baltic? It is said the Africans are idle, but they are not too idle, at least, to catch one another; seven hundred to one thousand tons of rice are annually bought of them; by the same rule why should we not buy more? At Gambia one thousand of them are seen continually at work; why should not some more thousands be set to work in the same manner? It is the slave trade that causes their idleness and every other mischief. We are told by one witness: 'They sell one another as they can', and while they can get brandy by catching one another, no wonder they are too idle for any regular work.

I have one word more to add upon a most material point but it is a point so self-evident that I shall be extremely short. It will appear from everything which I have said, that it is not regulation, it is not mere palliatives, that can cure this enormous evil. Total abolition is the only possible cure for it. The Jamaica report, indeed, admits much of the evil, but recommends it to us so to regulate the trade, that no persons should be kidnapped or made slaves contrary to the custom of Africa. But may they not be made slaves unjustly, and yet by no means contrary to the custom of Africa? I have shown they may, for all the customs of Africa are rendered savage and unjust through the influence of this trade; besides, how can we discriminate between the slaves justly and unjustly made? or, if we could, does any man believe that the British captains can, by any regulation in this country, be prevailed upon to refuse all such slaves as have not been fairly, honestly, and uprightly enslaved? But granting even that they should do this, yet how would the rejected slaves be recompensed? They are brought, as we are told, from three or four thousand miles off, and exchanged like cattle from one hand to another, until they reach the coast. We see then that it is the existence of the slave trade that is the spring of all this internal traffic, and that the remedy cannot be applied without abolition. Again, as to the middle passage, the evil is radical there also; the merchant's profit depends upon the number that can be crowded together, and upon the shortness of their allowance. Astringents, escarotis, and all the other arts of making them up for sale, are of the very essence of the trade; these arts will be concealed both from the purchaser and the legislature; they are necessary to the owner's profit, and they will be practised. Again, chains and arbitrary treatment must be used in transporting them; our seamen must be taught to play the tyrant, and that depravation of manners among them (which some very judicious persons have treated of as the very worst part of the business) cannot be hindered, while the trade itself continues. As to the slave merchants, they have already told you that if two slaves to a ton are not permitted, the trade cannot continue; so that the objections are done away by themselves on this quarter; and in the West Indies, I have shown that the abolition is the only possible stimulus whereby regard to population, and consequently to the happiness of the Negroes, can be effectually excited in those islands.

I trust, therefore, I have shown that upon every ground the total abolition ought to take place. I have urged many things which are not my own leading motives for proposing it, since I have wished to show every description of gentlemen, and particularly the West India planters, who deserve every attention, that the abolition is politic upon their own principles also. Policy, however sir, is not my principle, and I am not ashamed to say it. There is a principle above everything that is political; and when I reflect on the command which says: 'Thou shalt do no murder,' believing the authority to be divine, how can I dare to set up any reasonings of my own against it? And, sir, when we think of eternity, and of the future consequences of all human conduct, what is there in this life that should make any man contradict the dictates of his conscience, the principles of justice, the laws of religion, and of God? Sir, the nature and all the circumstances of this trade are now laid open to us; we can no longer plead ignorance, we cannot evade it, it is now an object placed before us, we cannot pass it; we may spurn it, we may kick it out of our way, but we cannot turn aside so as to avoid seeing it; for it is brought now so directly before our eyes that this House must decide, and must justify to all the world, and to their own consciences, the rectitude of the grounds and principles of their decision. A society has been established for the abolition of this trade, in which Dissenters, Quakers, churchmen – in which the most conscientious of all persuasions have all united, and made a common cause in this great question. Let not Parliament be the only body that is insensible to the principles of national justice. Let us make reparation to Africa, so far as we can, by establishing a trade upon true commercial principles, and we shall soon find the rectitude of our conduct rewarded by the benefits of a regular and a growing commerce.

William Wilberforce, 12 May 1789

The abolition of the slavery in Britain was not achieved until 1806, and it was not until 1833 – the year Wilberforce died – that, largely through his efforts, slavery and the slave trade was abolished throughout the British Empire.

Frederick Douglass escaped from slavery in the United States and spent two years in England in order to avoid capture by his former owners. He devoted his time to study, addressing meetings and writing his autobiography. On his return to the States he became the leading black abolitionist in the years before the Civil War. This speech was daringly delivered in Rochester, New York on 4 July 1852, nine years before the outbreak of the appalling conflict between the Northern and Southern States.

Fellow citizens, above your national, tumultuous joy, I hear the mournful wail of millions! whose chains, heavy and grievous yesterday, are, today, rendered more intolerable by the jubilee shouts that reach them. If I do forget, if I do not faithfully remember those bleeding children of sorrow this day, 'may my right hand forget her cunning, and may my tongue cleave to the roof of my mouth'! To forget them, to pass lightly over their wrongs, and to chime in with the popular theme would be treason most scandalous and shocking, and would make me a reproach before God and the world.

My subject, then, fellow citizens, is American slavery. I shall see this day and its popular characteristics from the slave's point of view. Standing there identified with the American bondman, making his wrongs mine. I do not hesitate to declare with all my soul that the character and conduct of this nation never looked blacker to me than on this Fourth of July! Whether we turn to the declarations of the past or to the professions of the present, the conduct of the nation seems equally hideous and revolting. America is false to the past, false to the present, and solemnly binds herself to be false to the future. Standing with God and the crushed and bleeding slave on this occasion, I will, in the name of humanity which is outraged, in the name of liberty which is fettered, in the name of the Constitution and the Bible which are disregarded and trampled upon, dare to call in question and to denounce, with all the emphasis I can command, everything that serves to perpetuate slavery – the great sin and shame of America! 'I will not equivocate; I will not excuse'; I will use the severest language I can command; and yet not one word shall escape me that any man, whose judgement is not blinded by prejudice, or who is not at heart a slaveholder, shall not confess to be right and just.

But I fancy I hear someone of my audience say, 'It is just in this circumstance that you and your brother abolitionists fail to make a favorable impression on the public mind. Would you argue more and denounce less, would you persuade more and rebuke less, your cause would be much more likely to succeed.' But, I submit, where all is plain there is nothing to be argued. What point in the anti-slavery creed would you have me argue? On what branch of the subject do the people of this country need light? Must I undertake to prove that the slave is a man? That point is conceded already. Nobody doubts it. The slaveholders themselves acknowledge it in the enactment of laws for their government. They acknowledge it when they punish disobedience on the part of the slave. There are seventy-two crimes in the state of Virginia which, if committed by a black man (no matter how ignorant he be), subject him to the punishment of death; while only two of the same crimes will subject a white man to the like punishment. What is this but the acknowledgement that the slave is a moral, intellectual, and responsible being? The manhood of the slave is conceded. It is admitted in the fact that Southern statute books are covered with enactments forbidding, under severe fines and penalties, the teaching of the slave to read or to write. When you can point to any such laws in reference to the beasts of the field, then I may consent to argue the manhood of the slave. When the dogs in your streets, when the fowls of the air, when the cattle on your hills, when the fish of the sea and the reptiles that crawl shall be unable to distinguish the slave from a brute, then will I argue with you that the slave is a man!

For the present, it is enough to affirm the equal manhood of the Negro race. Is it not astonishing that, while we are ploughing, planting, and reaping, using all kinds of mechanical tools, erecting houses, constructing bridges, building ships, working in metals of brass, iron, copper, silver and gold; while we are reading, writing, and ciphering, acting as clerks, merchants, and secretaries, having among us lawyers, doctors, ministers, poets, authors, editors, orators, and teachers; that while we are engaged in all manner of enterprises common to other men, capturing the whale in the Pacific, feeding sheep and cattle on the hillside, living, moving, acting, thinking, planning, living in families as husbands, wives and children and above all, confessing and worshipping the Christian's God, and looking hopefully for life and immortality beyond the grave, we are called upon to prove that we are men!

Would you have me argue that man is entitled to liberty? that he is the rightful owner of his own body? You have already declared it. Must I argue the wrongfulness of slavery? Is that a question for republicans? Is it to be settled by the rules of logic and argument-ation, as a matter beset with great difficulty, involving a doubtful application of the principle of justice, hard to be understood? How should I look today, in the presence of Americans, dividing and subdividing a discourse, to show that men have a natural right to freedom? speaking of it relatively and positively, negatively and affirmatively? To do so would be to make myself ridiculous and to offer an insult to your understanding. There is not a man beneath the canopy of heaven that does not know that slavery is wrong for him.

What, am I to argue that it is wrong to make men brutes, to rob them of their liberty, to work them without wages, to keep them ignorant of their relations to their fellow men, to beat them with sticks, to flay their flesh with the lash, to load their limbs with irons, to hunt them with dogs, to sell them at auction, to sunder their families, to knock out their teeth, to burn their flesh, to starve them into obedience and submission to their masters? Must I argue that a system thus marked with blood, and stained with pollution, is wrong? No! I will not. I have better employment for my time and strength than such arguments would imply.

What, then, remains to be argued? Is it that slavery is not divine; that God did not establish it; that our doctors of divinity are mis-taken? There is blasphemy in the thought. That which is inhuman cannot be divine! Who can reason on such a proposition? They that can may; I cannot. The time for such argument is past.

11

At a time like this, scorching iron, not convincing argument, is needed. O! had I the ability, and could I reach the nation's ear, I would today pour out a fiery stream of biting ridicule, blasting reproach, withering sarcasm, and stern rebuke. For it is not light that is needed, but fire; it is not the gentle shower, but thunder. We need the storm, the whirlwind, and the earthquake. The feeling of the nation must be quickened; the conscience of the nation must be roused; the propriety of the nation must be stated; the hypocrisy of the nation must be exposed; and its crimes against God and man must be proclaimed and denounced.

What, to the American slave, is your Fourth of July? I answer: a day that reveals to him, more than all other days in the year, the gross injustice and cruelty to which he is the constant victim. To him, your celebration is a sham; your boasted liberty, an unholy license; your national greatness, swelling vanity; your sounds of rejoicing are empty and heartless; your denunciation of tyrants, brass-fronted impudence; your shouts of liberty and equality, hollow mockery; your prayers and hymns, your sermons and thanksgivings, with all your religious parade and solemnity, are, to him, mere bombast, fraud, deception, impiety, and hypocrisy – a thin veil to cover up crimes which would disgrace a nation of savages. There is not a nation of savages. There is not a nation on the earth guilty of practices more shocking and bloody than are the people of the United States at this very hour.

Go where you may, search where you will, roam through all the monarchies and despotisms of the Old World, travel through South America, search out every abuse, and when you have found the last, lay your facts by the side of the everyday practices of this nation, and you will say with me that, for revolting barbarity and shameless hypocrisy, America reigns without a rival.

You boast of your love of liberty, your superior civilisation, and pure Christianity, while the whole political power of the nation, (as embodied in the two great political parties,) is solemnly pledged to support and perpetrate the enslavement of three millions of your countrymen. You hurl your anathemas at the crown-headed tyrants of Russia and Austria and pride yourselves on your democratic institutions, while you yourselves consent to be the mere tools and bodyguards of the tyrants of Virginia and Carolina.

You invite to your shores fugitives of oppression from abroad, honor them with banquets, greet them with ovations, cheer them, toast them, salute them, protect them, and pour out your money to them like water, but the fugitive from your own land you advertise, hunt, arrest, shoot and kill. You glory in your refinement and your universal education; yet you maintain a system as barbarous and dreadful as ever stained the character of a nation – a system begun in avarice, supported in pride, and perpetuated in cruelty.

You shed tears over fallen Hungary, and make the sad story of her wrongs the theme of your poets, statesmen and orators, till your gallant sons are ready to fly to arms to vindicate her cause against the oppressor; but in regard to the ten thousand wrongs of the American slave, you would enforce the strictest silence, and would hail him as an enemy of the nation who dares to make these wrongs the subject of public discourse!

Frederick Douglass (1815–95)

2. Cars

Geoffrey said, 'People like you and me are the best example of how too many cars isolate people. You can't use a bus, it's tough to get on a train, a lot of taxis can't take chairs, and that's because all anybody cares about is cars, cars, bloody cars.'

'Yes but I'm disabled Geoffrey, remember? Not everyone is like me.'

'Everybody is disabled by cars!' insisted Geoffrey.

'Geoffrey excuse me, but did you leave a door open in your brain here? Cars carry people around you know? They don't disable people, they *enable* them to get around – especially people like me. What's more, if you were rich you could buy me a great big car, a limmo with a chair lift and a chauffeur and a bar and a swimming pool. So just cut the philosophy OK? and hurry up and reinvent your stupid engine because the sooner I'm outta my converted Ford and into a stretch Mercedes the better.'

And with that, Deborah wheeled herself into the kitchen and filled the kettle from the hose attached to her tap. Her kettle could not move because it was attached to a clever little tilting platform that made pouring easier. Geoffrey followed Deborah into the kitchen.

'Do cars enable the woman with a ton of shopping waiting at the bus stop for the bus that never comes?' he shouted.

'So now he's onto Communism already,' said an exasperated Deborah struggling with the lid of a new coffee jar that would have given Mr. Universe a limp wrist. 'They tried Communism in Russia, Geoffrey. Their buses were worse than ours and everybody had to eat cabbage for the rest of their lives.'

Geoffrey would not be side-tracked by red, red herrings.

'Do cars *enable* the people who live on main routes and have to listen to traffic all night? Do they enable old people who can't cross roads, or have to walk miles extra to find a crossing? Do they *enable* the five thousand people killed each year in Britain, or the forty thousand in the US? Above all Deborah, do they *enable* the hundreds of thousands of people stuck in jams every day? I mean do they really? or do people just think they do?'

Ben Elton, *Gridlock* (1991)

What Ford and Hitler started
The motor corporations
Appear to be completing,
Offering the ingenious defence
That 'accidents will happen'.

Carbon monoxide,
Since its victims offered least resistance,
Was the death-camp gas that first found Hitler's favour.
Now massive dosages of carbon monoxide
Are apathetically inhaled
Throughout a global Autoreich.

The new theatre of war
Presents itself as a place of leisured entertainment
But, like some benighted South American stadium
It conceals an unpublicised death-zone . . .

Seventeen million dead,
And counting.

More than twice the number in the death camps.

Eighteen times the count in Korea.

Seventeen Vietnams.

A hundred and thirty times the kill at Hiroshima.

Here I Stand

Eight thousand five hundred Ulsters.

The Hundred Years war in a week.
The crusades in under thirty seconds
A humdrum holocaust.
The Third World War nobody bothered to declare.

Heathcote Williams, *Autogeddon* (1991)

3. Freedom

❧❦❧ ❧❦❧ ❧❦❧ ❧❦❧ ❧❦❧ ❧❦❧

'I Have a Dream'

. . . I say to you today, my friends, that in spite of the difficulties and frustrations of the moment I still have a dream. It is a dream deeply rooted in the American dream.

I have a dream that one day this nation will rise up and live out the true meaning of its creed: 'We hold these truths to be self-evident; that all men are created equal.'

I have a dream that one day on the red hills of Georgia the sons of former slaves and the sons of former slave owners will be able to sit down together at the table of brotherhood.

I have a dream that one day even the state of Mississippi, a desert state sweltering with the heat of injustice and oppression, will be transformed into an oasis of freedom and justice.

I have a dream that my four little children will one day live in a nation where they will not be judged by the color of their skin but by the content of their character.

I have a dream today.

I have a dream that one day the state of Alabama, whose governor's lips are presently dripping with the words of interposition and nullification, will be transformed into a situation where little black boys and black girls will be able to join hands with little white boys and girls and walk together as sisters and brothers.

I have a dream today.

I have a dream that one day every valley shall be exalted, every hill and mountain shall be made low, the rough places will be made plain, and the crooked places will be made straight, and the glory of the Lord shall be revealed, and all flesh shall see it together.

This is our hope. This is the faith with which I return to the South. With this faith we will be able to hew out of the mountain of despair a stone of hope. With this faith we will be able to transform the jangling discords of our nation into a beautiful symphony of brotherhood.

With this faith we will be able to work together, to pray together, to struggle together, to go to jail together, to stand up for freedom together, knowing that we will be free one day.

This will be the day when all of God's children will be able to sing with new meaning.

> My country 'tis of thee,
> Sweet land of liberty,
>   of thee I sing:
> Land where my father died,
> Land of the Pilgrims' pride,
> From every mountainside
>   Let freedom ring.

And if America is to be a great nation, this must become true.
So let freedom ring from the prodigious hilltops of New Hampshire.
Let freedom ring from the mighty mountains of New York.
Let freedom ring from the heightening Alleghenies of Pennsylvania!
Let freedom ring from the snowcapped Rockies of Colorado!
Let freedom ring from the curvaceous peaks of California.
But not only that; let freedom ring from Stone Mountain of Georgia!
Let freedom ring from Lookout Mountain of Tennessee!
Let freedom ring from every hill and molehill of Mississippi.
From every mountainside, let freedom ring.

When we let freedom ring, when we let it ring from every village and every hamlet, from every state and every city, we will be able to speed up that day when all of God's children, black men and white men, Jews and Gentiles, Protestants and Catholics, will be able to join hands and sing in the words of the old Negro spiritual, 'Free at last! Free at last! Thank God Almighty, we are free at last!'

The Revd Dr Martin Luther King Jnr, Washington, 28 August 1963

4. Guns

Perhaps it's not altogether surprising that, with a wife who is Commander in Chief of the British Armed Forces whose nuclear missiles can, within minutes, wipe out several cities the size of London, Prince Philip has a rather dismissive view of guns – in comparison they are pretty small beer.

'. . . *if a cricketer suddenly decided to go into a school*', said Philip in a recent radio interview, *'and battered a lot of people to death with a cricket bat which he could do very easily, I mean are you going to ban cricket bats?*' That's about as sophisticated as the 'guns debate' had got. Supporters of gun control were outraged while the pro-shooting lobby congratulated the Duke for his 'courage' in speaking out.

Of course it's true that guns like cricket bats, or the 'impossible'-to-define knives, are all inanimate objects and left lying about will cause little harm; to turn them into lethal 'weapons' requires a little human help. This, essentially, is the only, non-commercial, non-selfish argument which underpins the gun lobby – guns don't kill, people do. In some respects this is a more accurate assessment of the situation than that offered by some supporters of gun-control, until, that is, we understand that we humans can kill, by touching the trigger.

You will not be surprised to know that I have not been able to find a single case of anyone, anywhere in the world going on a murderous rampage in a school or anywhere else, with a cricket bat, while instances of murderous use of guns, even if one leaves out wars, are legion. There is a good reason for this which seems to have escaped the good prince.

The significant difference between a cricket bat and a gun is

20

that one was devised for playing a game, not smashing people's heads, while the other was designed and refined over the years for one purpose only – to kill. This is the meaning and significance that any gun, however it is used or whatever drawer or holster it is left in, carries with it and that is why it is a weapon of choice for any practical person. One may be able to garrotte people with a knife, smash heads with golf clubs and kill people with motor cars but these are incidental uses of tools created for other quite reasonable purposes – such is life. But a gun or any representation of a gun, unlike a cricket bat, carries with it and passes on to the owner an element of its murderous origins and its bloody history. Guns were not devised for defence, on the contrary they were the tools of tyrants and megalomaniacs who robbed and murdered for self aggrandisement.

An acceptance of a gun or its representation into our lives is an acceptance of the legitimacy of its purpose. Whether it is the police, the shooters or children with their toy guns or their fantastic and futuristic variants, the embodied message in the guns and toys is that killing to get one's way is acceptable. Though none of this seems to have turned us into a country of deranged murderers.

Half a million children, according to a recent World Health Organisation report, have died in Iraq as a result of the Gulf War in which British armed forces, with wide popular public support were major participants. Few people in Britain pulled any trigger but the majority gave legitimacy to Desert Storm and all that followed. In legal terms this is not murder but beside this what happened in Dunblane pales into insignificance. The killing and misery in Dunblane was apparently caused by an unbalanced individual whilst the deaths in Iraq were caused by apparently sane and well-balanced people. No doubt the Duke has a sporting explanation.

Jan Melichar, editor of *Peace Matters*, the quarterly magazine of the Peace Pledge Union, Winter 1996/1997

5. Human Rights

Thomas Paine, an Englishman who had emigrated to America, where he had worked as a journalist and fought against the British in the American revolutionary war, after visiting France returned to England where he published The Rights of Man, *a reply to Edmund Burke's* Reflections on the Revolution in France. The Rights of Man *not only supported the French Revolution, it also argued in favour of a Republican system of government in Britain and the dissolution of the British monarchy.*

A warrant for Paine's arrest, on a charge of treason, was issued and Paine fled to France. He was tried in absentia by a special jury of the Court of the King's Bench. He was defended by a very prominent lawyer, Thomas Erskine, who was sympathetic towards the French Revolution. It is said that Erskine's defence of Paine curtailed his career prospects within the English judiciary.

The 'trial' was in fact a mere formality. As the Attorney General rose to reply to Erskine's speech, the foreman of the jury declared that the jury, without need for discussion, had reached its verdict, and the verdict was 'Guilty'. In the light of Erskine's eloquent defence of the right to freedom of opinion within the law, the jury's action clearly demonstrated that a form of 'praejudicium', or preconceived judgment, had been agreed. In ancient Rome, 'praejudicium' was the form of judgment which rightly became the basis of the word 'prejudiced'.

Here is Thomas Erskine's defence of Thomas Paine.

I say, in the name of Thomas Paine, and in his words as author of *The Rights of Man* as written in the very volume that is charged with seeking the destruction of property;

The end of all political associations is the preservation of the rights of man, which rights are liberty, property, and security; that the nation is the source of all sovereignty derived from it; the right of property being secured and inviolable, no one ought to be deprived of it, except in cases of evident public necessity, legally ascertained, and on condition of a previous, just indemnity.

These are undoubtedly the rights of man – the rights for which all governments are established – and the only rights Mr Paine contends for; but which he thinks (no matter whether right or wrong) are better to be secured by a republican Constitution than by the forms of the English government. He instructs me to admit that, when government is once constituted, no individuals, without rebellion, can withdraw their obedience from it – that all attempts to excite them to it are highly criminal, for the most obvious reason of policy and justice – that nothing short of the will of a whole people can change or affect the rule by which a nation is to be governed – and that no private opinion, however honestly inimical to the forms or substance of the law, can justify resistance to its authority, while it remains in force. The author of *The Rights of Man* not only admits the truth of all this doctrine, but he consents to be convicted, and I also consent for him, unless his work shall be found studiously and painfully to inculcate these great principles of government which it is charged to have been written to destroy.

Let me not, therefore, be suspected to be contending that it is lawful to write a book pointing out defects in the English government, and exciting individuals to destroy its sanctions and to refuse obedience. But, on the other hand, I do contend that it is lawful to address the English nation on these momentous subjects; for had it not been for this inalienable right (thanks be to God and our fathers for establishing it!), how should we have had this Constitution which we so loudly boast of? If, in the march of the human mind, no man could have gone before the establishments of the time he lived in, how could our establishment, by reiterated changes, have become what it is? If no man could have awakened the public mind to errors and abuses in our government, how could it have passed on from stage to stage, through reformation and revolution, so as to have arrived from barbarism to such a pitch of happiness and perfection that the Attorney-General considers it a profanation to touch it further or to look for any future amendment?

In this manner power has reasoned in every age – government, in its own estimation, has been at all times a system of perfection; but a free press has examined and detected its errors, and the people have, from time to time, reformed them. This freedom has alone made our government what it is; this freedom alone can preserve it; and therefore, under the banners of that freedom, today I stand up to defend Thomas Paine. But how, alas! shall this task be accomplished? How may I expect from you what human nature has not made man for the performance of? How am I to address your reasons, or ask them to pause, amidst the torrent of prejudice which has hurried away the public mind on the subject you are to judge? . . .

Was any Englishman ever so brought as a criminal before an English court of justice? If I were to ask you, gentlemen of the jury, what is the choicest fruit that grows upon the tree of English liberty, you would answer: security under the law. If I were to ask the whole people of England the return they looked for at the hands of the government, for the burdens under which they bend to support it, I should still be answered: security under the law; or, in other words, an impartial administration of justice. So sacred, therefore, has the freedom of trial been ever held in England – so anxiously does Justice guard against every possible bias in her path – that if the public mind has been locally agitated upon any subject in judgement, the forum has either been changed or the trial postponed. The circulation of any paper that brings, or can be supposed to bring, prejudice, or even well-founded knowledge, within the reach of a British tribunal, on the spur of an occasion, is not only highly criminal, but defeats itself, by leading to put off the trial which its object was to pervert . . .

Milton wisely says that a disposition in a nature to this species of controversy is no proof of sedition or degeneracy, but quite the reverse (I omitted to cite the passage with the others). In speaking of this subject, he rises into that inexpressibly sublime style of writing wholly peculiar to himself, he was, indeed, no plagiary from anything human; he looked up for light and expression, as he himself wonderfully describes it, by devout prayer to that great Being who is the source of all utterance and knowledge, and who sendeth out His seraphim with the hallowed fire of His altar to touch and purify the lips of whom He pleases. 'When the cheerfulness of the people,' says this mighty poet, 'is so sprightly up, as that it hath not only wherewith to guard well its own freedom and safety, but to spare, and to bestow upon the solidest and sublimest points of controversy and new invention, it betokens us not degenerated nor drooping to a fatal decay, but casting off the old and wrinkled skin of corruption, to outlive these pangs and wax young again, entering the glorious ways of truth and prosperous virtue, destined to become great and honourable in these latter ages. Methinks I see in my mind a noble and puissant nation rousing herself, like a strong man after sleep, and shaking her invincible locks; methinks I see her as an eagle mewing her mighty youth, and kindling her undazzled eyes at the full midday beam; purging and unsealing her long-abused sight at the fountain itself of heavenly radiance; while the whole noise of timorous and flocking birds, with those also that love the twilight, flutter about, amazed at what she means, and in their envious gabble would prognosticate a year of sects and schisms.'

Gentlemen, what Milton only saw in his mighty imagination, I see in fact; what he expected, but which never came to pass, I see now fulfilling; methinks I see this noble and puissant nation, not degenerated and drooping to a fatal decay, but casting off the wrinkled skin of corruption to put on again the vigour of her youth. And it is because others as well as myself see this that we have all this uproar. France and its Constitution are the mere pretences. It is because Britons begin to recollect the inheritance of their own Constitution left them by their ancestors; it is because they are awakened to the corruptions which have fallen upon its most valuable parts, that forsooth the nation is in danger of being destroyed by a single pamphlet . . .

Gentlemen, I have but a few more words to trouble you with: I take my leave of you with declaring that all this freedom which I have been endeavouring to assert is no more than the ancient freedom which belongs to our own inbred Constitution; I have not asked you to acquit Thomas Paine upon any new lights, or upon any principle but that of the law, which you are sworn to administer – my great object has been to inculcate that wisdom and policy which are the parents of the government of Great Britain, forbid this jealous eye over her subjects; and that, on the contrary, they cry aloud in the language of the poet, adverted to by Lord Chatham on the memorable subject of America, unfortunately without effect.

> Be to their faults a little blind
> Be to their virtues a little kind
> Let all their thoughts be unconfin'd
> Nor clap your padlock on the mind.

Engage the people by their affections, convince their reason – and they will be loyal from the only principle that can make loyalty sincere, vigorous, or rational – a conviction that it is their truest interest, and that their government is for their good. Constraint is the natural parent of resistance, and a pregnant proof that reason is not on the side of those who use it. You must all remember Lucian's pleasant story: Jupiter and a countryman were walking together, conversing with great freedom and familiarity upon the subject of heaven and earth. The countryman listened with attention and acquiescence, while Jupiter strove only to convince him – but happening to hint a doubt, Jupiter turned hastily around and threatened him with his thunder. 'Ah! ah!' says the countryman, 'now, Jupiter, I know that you are wrong; you are always wrong when you appeal to your thunder.'

This is the case with me – I can reason with the people of England, but I cannot fight against the thunder of authority.

Gentlemen, this is my defence of free opinions. With regard to myself, I am, and always have been, obedient and affectionate to the law – to that rule of action, as long as I exist, I shall ever do as I have done today, maintain the dignity of my high profession, and perform, as I understand them, all its important duties.

Thomas Erskine, 18 December 1792

6. Medical Ethics

❧❦❧ ❧❦❧ ❧❦❧ ❧❦❧ ❧❦❧ ❧❦❧

The Hippocratic Oath

I swear by Apollo the healer, invoking all the gods and goddesses to be my witnesses, that I will fulfil this Oath and this written Covenant to the best of my ability and judgement.

I will look upon him who shall have taught me this Art even as one of my own parents. I will share my substance with him, and I will supply his necessities, if he be in need. I will regard his offspring even as my own brethren, and I will teach them this Art, if they would learn it, without fee or covenant. I will impart this Art by precept, by lecture and by every mode of teaching, not only to my own sons but to the sons of him who taught me, and to disciples bound by covenant and oath, according to the Law of Medicine.

The regimen I adopt shall be for the benefit of the patients according to my ability and judgement, and not for their hurt or for any wrong. I will give no deadly drug to any, though it be asked of me, nor will I counsel such, and especially I will not aid a woman to procure abortion. Whatsoever house I enter, there will I go for the benefit of the sick, refraining from all wrongdoing or corruption, and especially from any art of seduction, of male or female, of bond or free. Whatsoever things I see or hear concerning the life of men, in my attendance on the sick or even apart therefrom, which ought not to be noised abroad, I will keep silence thereon, counting such things to be as sacred secrets. Pure and holy will I keep my Life and my Art.

If I fulfil this Oath and confound it not, be it mine to enjoy

Life and Art alike, with good repute among all men at all times. If I transgress and violate my oath, may the reverse be my lot.

Geneva Convention – Code of Medical Ethics

(adopted by the World Medical Association in 1949)

> I solemnly pledge myself to consecrate my life to the service of humanity;
> I will give to my teachers the respect and gratitude which is their due;
> I will practice my profession with conscience and dignity;
> The health of my patient will be my first consideration;
> I will respect the secrets which are confided in me;
> I will maintain by all the means in my power, the honour and the noble traditions of the medical profession;
> My colleagues will be my brothers;
> I will not permit considerations of religion, nationality, race, party politics or social standing to intervene between my duty and my patient.
> I will maintain the utmost respect for human life from the time of conception; even under threat.
> I will not use my medical knowledge contrary to the laws of humanity.
> I make these promises solemnly, freely and upon my honour.

Human Biomedical Research

World Medical Association

The Helsinki Declaration, for the guidance of doctors in biomedical research involving human subjects, was adopted by the World Medical Assembly 1964, revised 1975.

Introduction

It is the mission of the medical doctor to safeguard the health of the people. His or her knowledge and conscience are dedicated to the fulfilment of this mission.

The Declaration of Geneva of The World Medical Association binds the doctor with the words, 'The health of my patient will be my first consideration,' and the International Code of Medical Ethics declares that, 'Any act or advice which could weaken physical or mental resistance of a human being may be used only in his interest.'

The purpose of biomedical research involving human subjects must be to improve diagnostic, therapeutic and prophylactic procedures and the understanding of the aetiology and pathogenesis of disease.

In current medical practice most diagnostic, therapeutic or prophylactic procedures involve hazards. This applies *a fortiori* to biomedical research.

Medical progress is based on research which ultimately must rest in part on experimentation involving human subjects.

In the field of biomedical research a fundamental distinction must be recognised between medical research in which the aim is essentially diagnostic or therapeutic for a patient, and medical research, the essential object of which is purely scientific and without direct diagnostic or therapeutic value to the person subjected to the research. Special caution must be exercised in the conduct of research which may affect the environment, and the welfare of animals used for research must be respected. Because it is essential that the results of laboratory experiments be applied to human beings to further scientific knowledge and to help suffering humanity, The World Medical Association has prepared the following recommendations as a guide to every doctor in biomedical research involving human subjects. They should be kept under review in the future. It must be stressed that the standards as drafted are only a guide to physicians all over the world. Doctors are not relieved from criminal, civil and ethical responsibilities under the laws of their own countries.

(i) Basic principles

1. Biomedical research involving human subjects must conform

to generally accepted scientific principles and should be based on adequately performed laboratory and animal experimentation and on a thorough knowledge of the scientific literature.

2. The design and performance of each experimental procedure involving human subjects should be clearly formulated in an experimental protocol which should be transmitted to a specially appointed independent committee for consideration, comment and guidance.

3. Biomedical research involving human subjects should be conducted only by scientifically qualified persons and under the supervision of a clinically competent medical person. The responsibility for the human subject must always rest with a medically qualified person and never rest on the subject of research, even though the subject has given his or her consent.

4. Biomedical research involving human subjects cannot legitimately be carried out unless the importance of the objective is in proportion to the inherent risk to the subject.

5. Every biomedical research project involving human subjects should be preceded by careful assessment of predictable risks in comparison with foreseeable benefits to the subject or to others. Concern for the interests of the subject must always prevail over the interests of science and society.

6. The right of the research subject to safeguard his or her integrity must always be respected. Every precaution should be taken to respect the privacy of the subject and to minimise the impact of the study on the subject's physical and mental integrity and on the personality of the subject.

7. Doctors should abstain from engaging in research projects involving human subjects unless they are satisfied that the hazards involved are believed to be predictable. Doctors should cease any investigation if the hazards are found to outweigh the potential benefits.

8. In publication of the results of his or her research, the doctor is obliged to preserve the accuracy of the results. Reports of experimentation not in accordance with the principles laid down in this Declaration should not be accepted for publication.

9. In any research on human beings, each potential subject must be adequately informed of the aims, methods, anticipated benefits and potential hazards of the study and the discomfort it may entail. He or she should be informed that he or she is at liberty to abstain from participation in the study and that he or she is free to withdraw his or her consent to participation at any time. The doctor should then obtain the subject's freely-given informed consent, preferably in writing.

10. When obtaining informed consent for the research project the doctor should be particularly cautious if the subject is in a dependent relationship to him or her or may consent under duress. In that case the informed consent should be obtained by a doctor who is not engaged in the investigation and who is completely independent of this official relationship.

11. In case of legal incompetence, informed consent should be obtained from the legal guardian in accordance with national legislation. Where physical or mental incapacity makes it impossible to obtain informed consent, or when the subject is a minor, permission from the responsible relative replaces that of the subject in accordance with national legislation.

12. The research protocol should always contain a statement of the ethical considerations involved and should indicate that the principles enunciated in the present Declaration are complied with.

(ii) Medical research combined with professional care (clinical research)

1. In the treatment of the sick person, the doctor must be free to use a new diagnostic and therapeutic measure, if in his or her

judgement it offers hope of saving life, re-establishing health or alleviating suffering.

2. The potential benefits, hazards and discomfort of a new method should be weighed against the advantages of the best current diagnostic and therapeutic methods.

3. In any medical study, every patient – including those of a control group, if any – should be assured of the best proven diagnostic and therapeutic method.

4. The refusal of the patient to participate in a study must never interfere with the doctor-patient relationship.

5. If the doctor considers it essential not to obtain informed consent, the specific reasons for this proposal should be stated in the experimental protocol for transmission to the independent committee.

6. The doctor can combine medical research with professional care, the objective being the acquisition of new medical knowledge, only to the extent that the medical research is justified by its potential diagnostic or therapeutic value for the patient.

(iii) Non-therapeutic biomedical research involving human subjects (non-clinical biomedical research)

1. In the purely scientific application of medical research carried out on a human being, it is the duty of the doctor to remain the protector of the life and health of that person on whom biomedical research is being carried out.

2. The subjects should be volunteers – either healthy persons or patients for whom the experimental design is not related to the patient's illness.

3. The investigator or the investigating team should discontinue the research if in his/her or their judgement it may, if continued, be harmful to the individual.

4. In research on humans, the interest of science and society should never take precedence over considerations related to the well-being of the subject.

Suicide

Man is a prisoner who has no right to open the door of his prison and run away.

Plato (428–348 BC)

There is no suicide for which all society is not responsible.

Cyril Connolly (1903–74)

> To be, or not to be, – that is the question –
> Whether 'tis nobler in the mind to suffer
> The slings and arrows of outrageous fortune,
> Or to take arms against a sea of troubles,
> And by opposing end them? – To die, – to sleep, –
> No more; and by a sleep to say we end
> The heart-ache and the thousand natural shocks
> That flesh is heir to, – 'tis a consummation
> Devoutly to be wish'd. To die, – to sleep; –
> To sleep! perchance to dream: – ay, there's the rub;
> For in that sleep of death what dreams may come,
> When we have shuffled off this mortal coil,
> Must give us pause: there's the respect
> That makes calamity of so long life;
> For who would bear the whips and scorns of time,
> The oppressor's wrong, the proud man's contumely,
> The pangs of despised love, the law's delay,
> The insolence of office, and the spurns
> That patient merit of the unworthy takes,
> When he himself might his quietus make
> With a bare bodkin? who would fardels bear,
> To grunt and sweat under a weary life,

But that the dread of something after death, –
The undiscover'd country, from whose bourn
No traveller returns, – puzzles the will,
And makes us rather bear those ills we have
Than fly to others that we know not of?
Thus conscience does make cowards of us all;
And thus the native hue of resolution
Is sicklied o'er with the pale cast of thought;
And enterprises of great pith and moment,
With this regard, their currents turn awry,
And lose the name of action.

William Shakespeare (1564–1616), *Hamlet* act 3, sc. 1

Suicide is no longer a crime, but to 'aid or abet' someone who wishes to commit suicide is a very serious crime. Medical practitioners sometimes have to negotiate an extremely fine line to keep within what may be described as 'ethically and legally correct conduct' in the treatment of, say, a severely disabled, or very low weight newborn baby, or a terminally ill adult enduring an abysmally poor quality of life. Such situations frequently present dilemmas to which the answers are not immediately obvious or crystal-clear.

A respectable ethical argument can, I submit, be made for not striving to keep alive those babies who soon after birth can be shown to have no capacity ever to flourish as human beings. Modern medicine has brought us to the point where almost all babies are salvageable in some form. But simply because we can salvage them does not mean that we must. We have never as a society regarded the preservation of life as an absolute value in itself. We admit the notion of the just war, and we praise, rather than condemn, the hero who sacrifices his life in a good cause. We also concede that no one has an absolute right to life, since the just war may warrant life being taken, as may capital punishment or the action of a ship's captain in closing bulkheads to save his ship and its passengers, even though some crew on the wrong side of the bulkhead will drown. On the other hand, we do not think that life should be taken lightly. It is something of fundamental value to us. Thus, it should only be taken, or someone should only be left to die, if a very good reason exists. If you apply this reasoning to the new-born, you will see that, while he has no absolute right to life, he should be helped to live unless there is a very good reason to do otherwise. A demonstrable incapacity to flourish as a human being in the sense in which I have indicated would, in my view, amount to such a reason.

Once articulated, these ethical rules would apply equally to other situations in which the quality of life is an issue. For example, in the case of the terminally ill, they would offer a guide to the doctor as to whether he is ethically and legally obliged to intervene if, say, pneumonia or cardiac arrest strikes a patient with advanced cancer. If the patient is unconscious or so drugged, out of necessity, as to be out of contact with the world or is racked by pain, it could be said that his capacity to flourish as a human being has been lost. This would provide the justification for letting nature take its course.

What if someone not yet *in extremis* decides of his own volition that he wishes to die now, rather than await the degrading decline he fears? Do the principles we have begun to map out apply to him, such that if he is asked, his doctor may help him achieve death? The case of R.v. Reed serves as a caution. The British Euthanasia Society, Exit, is a society which exists to disseminate information to any of its members on how to take his life. In October 1991, the Secretary of the Society was convicted of the crime of aiding and abetting the suicide of several people, all of whom had contacted the Society since they were contemplating suicide, but were fearful that they might make a mess of things. He was sentenced to two and a half years in prison. Undoubtedly he broke the law. There was, however, no effort on the part of the judge to reshape the law, or to interpret it so as to avoid conviction. Further, the sentence was intended as a warning to others. I invite you to stand back and consider what this prosecution and conviction say about our society when contrasted with the case of Dr Arthur. [Acquitted of the charge of the murder of a three-day-old baby boy, Dr Arthur had engaged in a 'holding operation', keeping the baby comfortable and nursing and feeding the baby, but otherwise waiting to see whether he would rally and live or whether 'nature would take its course'. This, it was said, was proper conduct, both ethically and legally.]

Elderly and, in some cases, ill people formed an intention to kill themselves. They made an autonomous choice, for them, perhaps, the final act of self-determination. They feared, more than anything, ending their days in a hospital bed, shorn of any dignity, prevented from dying, the reluctant recipients of all that modern medicine can deliver. There can be no doubt that this is a very real fear for many, whether it is justified or not. So they sought advice and were given it. They chose to die. And their helper was sent to gaol.

Would it have made any difference if their helper had been a doctor? As a matter of legal principle, it would not. The aiding and abetting of suicide would still have been a crime. But in practice it would have made all the difference in the world. First, there would not have been the fanfare of publicity which surrounded Exit's activities, promoted in part by Exit. Instead, there would have been a discussion between doctor and patient. Second, the means chosen for the comfortable death would have been different: more subtle and more carefully managed. Third, the doctor would undoubtedly have been able to call on medical experts who could show that the dosage of drugs used was not outside the norm of treatment or did not cause or may not have caused the death. And so on. I have no doubt that many doctors have responded to requests for assistance, and have helped such patients ease their way towards death. I am not criticizing them. I believe it can be defended as a humane and caring act in certain, carefully limited circumstances. What is important here is to notice the ethical and legal implications of the Exit case. Surely what happened cannot be explained simply on the basis that in the Exit case there was no doctor. For doctors, as we have seen, enjoy no special privileges. But when a doctor stands by and allows a baby to die, because the child is disabled and unwanted, professionals are tumbling over themselves to defend him and to praise him (at least in public), and he is acquitted. But there was no question of any autonomous decision by the baby. He had no part in the proceedings. If we excuse those who choose death for babies, who cannot speak for themselves, we should, perhaps, be slow to punish those who facilitate the autonomous decision of someone to destroy himself. Alternatively, we must live with the charge of hypocrisy, or even one law for the professional and one for the rest.

Aiding Suicide

It may happen sometimes that the patient may wish to end his life, rather than wait for death. The specialists again argue that with the right regime of treatment, there is no need for this to happen; but in reality the right regime is not always available, and even if it were, some patients may wish to retain their independence to choose suicide. By the Suicide Act 1961 section 2, English law makes aiding and abetting the suicide of another a serious crime. Thus, a doctor is under a duty to refrain from any act which may aid his patient in committing suicide. It is, however, a fine line between aiding suicide and making available, for example, certain drugs to relieve pain which, if more than a certain dosage is taken, will cause death. A court would, I submit, be slow to find liable a doctor who merely facilitated the self-determination of someone unable through illness to help himself. This should be contrasted with the situation in which the patient instructs the doctor to refrain from further treatment. As has been seen, the doctor is under a duty to comply with this request, provided the patient is lucid and competent. This is not aiding a suicide, since the patient is not, I submit, committing suicide, but only declining further medical care.

Ian Kennedy, *Treat Me Right* (1991)

Euthanasia

In considering the mercy killing of patients, the spheres of law and morality must be distinguished, although it is evident that to some extent they overlap . . . as the law stands at present direct destruction of the life of a patient, whether or not he has requested it, is murder; and failure to institute life-saving measures might – depending on the circumstances – constitute culpable negligence.

Euthanasia legislation would remove certain instances of direct killing of patients from the category of murder. (Failure to carry out treatment would presumably continue to be assessed according to circumstances.)

Whether or not active euthanasia became legal, however, some points of view in ethics would regard it as always morally wrong. Theories which identify a moral law prohibiting 'killing of the innocent' (but not judicial killing of murderers or killing in a 'just war') place mercy killing in the same moral category as murder. Thus E. Welty, writing in *A Handbook of Christian Social Ethics* (1963, p. 130) states: '. . . no-one may ask for it, demand, order, suggest it or carry it out: it must be resolutely refused to the sick person (and his relatives), however intense his suffering, however small his hope of recovery.' Welty goes on to defend this absolute opposition to euthanasia with the argument that: 'It is not God's will, and is neither permitted to us mortals nor indeed possible for us, to strip death of all its terror and pain: death is meant to be the last and greatest test we have to undergo here on earth.'

At the opposite end of the spectrum, the most consistent versions of greatest happiness theory can raise no objection to ending lives which are of no use either to the individual or to society. Provided euthanasia were carefully controlled so that only really hopeless cases were included, social benefit would accrue from painlessly killing not only those with severe pain in terminal illness, but also the grossly deformed and the severely subnormal. Such euthanasia would have to be imposed in cases where consent could not be obtained, but, for the sake of maximising happiness and avoiding pain, this might be regarded as a praiseworthy act of mercy.

Between these two opposing attitudes, a shifting middle ground is occupied both by advocates of *voluntary* euthanasia and by those who, whilst preferring to retain legal sanctions against it, believe that in some instances a physician's conscience may lead him to disregard the law. The assumption shared by both of these approaches to the problem is that the integrity of persons may be more important than the sanctity of human life. The more 'conservative' of the two approaches allows direct attack on life only in exceptional circumstances, when all other measures to prevent suffering have failed. The more 'liberal' view believes that each person has a right to decide for himself that his life should be ended, if certain irremediable medical conditions ensue. If such a middle ground is sought, there are no simple answers to the euthanasia question. The choice would appear to be between the uncertainty of the present legal situation in which a patient's trust might be betrayed by too little, or too much, action by his doctor and in which a doctor may be forced to risk prosecution out of concern for his patient; and, on the other hand, the cold logic of a law which would formalise a situation whose essentials are trust and sensitivity to another's need. There is no doubting the awareness of suffering which motivates proposals for voluntary euthanasia. The problem is finding appropriate structures through which the rational and emotional aspects of compassion can be given expression.

It is at this point of the argument that moral law theory appears to come into its own. Advocates for voluntary euthanasia legisla-tion seem to underrate the exemplary character of the law. Much has been said . . . about the inflexible character of the legalist approach to morality, but the protective function of law should also be acknowledged. A legal system which enshrines the in-violability of human life (including the lives of those found guilty of murder) may appear to dispense rough justice to people who kill others with the best of motives. But the justice would be much rougher in a situation in which killing became legal. The burden of proof would then shift to the state to prove that a given instance of 'voluntary euthanasia' was a violation of law. For this reason the argument of natural law theorists that some moral rules have an absoluteness which protects human values carries considerable weight. It should be noted, however, that 'rule-utilitarianism' would draw a similar conclusion. Arguing from the standpoint of the security afforded to the majority by consistent laws against killing, it would acknowledge that in some instances the un-happiness of a minority may have to be accepted.

In any case, it often seems that intolerable distress and suffering in some terminal conditions have been too easily regarded as inevitable. A positive outcome of the campaign for voluntary euthanasia has been increased concern about developing new facilities for care of the dying and new techniques for relief of pain.

Alistair V. Campbell, *Moral Dilemmas in Medicine*

Abortion

Abortion Kills Children

Abortion is the deliberate killing of an unborn child. Abortion denies the most basic of human rights, the right to life, that is due in justice to all members of the human family.

The Humanity of the Unborn Child

Birth does not mark the beginning of a new life, but the emergence of that individual from the womb. A new life begins in the womb (usually in the womb's fallopian tube) when an ovum (egg) from the mother is fertilised by a single sperm from the father. At fertilisation (conception), a new, unique, living human individual is present.

The developing baby (called a *zygote* at the single cell stage, an *embryo* up to the end of the eighth week, and a *fetus* from nine weeks until birth,) is not part of the mother any more than he or she is part of the father. At conception all the hereditary characteristics of the new human being are established: eye colour, sex, build etc.

Nothing further is needed to direct the development of the embryo: all the information about how the baby is to grow and develop is contained in the original single cell at conception. Nothing is added after conception except oxygen and nutrients (food and water), the same essentials that are needed to sustain our life at all stages. From the beginning of the ninth week the term *fetus* is used to indicate that the developing child, whose body is now essentially complete, is recognisable to the eye as a human baby in miniature.

Birth is thus a change in the baby's environment, not a change in the nature of the baby. Humanity is not acquired but is inherent in all members of the human race.

. . . Not only is abortion a grave injustice in itself, it also perpetuates other social injustices. Abortion itself does not solve the social problems which lead women to seek abortions (such as unstable relationships, poor housing, and financial insecurity). Rather, it undermines the will of society – at the levels of family, peer group and government – to find human solutions which do not involve killing a baby.

Society for the Protection of Unborn Children, 1997

About two years ago I was attending a great Christian festival in Canada. As part of the proceedings they had what they called a market-place where various organizations connected with the churches were invited to display their wares and distribute their literature. Among the huge variety of agencies that applied for a stall were two that faced the organizing committee with a certain dilemma. On the one hand there was the pro-life campaign, a group strongly committed to the protection of the unborn child and therefore opposed to abortion in any form; and on the other there was a group that called themselves pro-choice, who argued that women should have the right to decide for themselves whether they would carry a baby to its full-term or not.

Both groups claimed to base their arguments on Christian principles. The pro-life protagonists could quote numerous scriptural passages attesting to the sacredness of human life within the womb; the pro-choice group argued that all human beings, and that must include women, have been entrusted by God with the responsibility of exercising their own free will.

The festival organizers were prepared to let both groups set up their stands and present their case, but at first neither was tolerant of the other's presence. However, when faced with the ultimatum that they either came together, or not at all, they reluctantly agreed to co-exist.

I visited both groups. I was deeply impressed by the literature produced as evidence against abortion, which was distributed by an energetic team of committed and convinced campaigners. The pro-choice lobbyists were not so forthcoming, and the reason for that became obvious when I eventually found their stall. To my surprise, it was staffed by a young woman who was herself heavily pregnant and who was spending her time contentedly knitting a matinee coat.

I told her I had expected a somewhat more militant feminist than so maternal a figure. She replied that she felt that motherhood was such an important vocation that it should only be entered upon willingly and responsibly. After all, she said, the 'Choice' can be 'Yes'. Even when the angel came to tell Mary that she had been chosen to be the mother of Jesus, we're told that Mary was allowed first to give her consent.

I've thought a lot about those two groups at the festival during this past weekend as the debate has raged about the child in Ireland made pregnant against her will. I have no doubt that abortion is an evil process and that it is right that there should be legislation to protect the unborn. But to my mind abortion is not more evil than rape. And there are times when the lesser evil has to be chosen for the sake of the greater good. In this, as in so many moral dilemmas, people will have sincere differences of view as to which is the lesser evil. But whatever verdict we arrive at we do well to heed the teaching of Jesus that above the compulsion of law we must always set the compassion of love.

Dr Pauline Webb, BBC *Thought for the Day*, 24 February 1992

Artificial Insemination

The air is suddenly thick with the sound of foetuses coming home to haunt the roost. A Dutch couple, Clemens and Sonja Peters, paid £12,000 'expenses' to surrogate mother Karen Roche to be artificially inseminated with Mr Peters' sperm and bear his child for them.

A gothic tragedy then unravelled. Mrs Roche first announced she had aborted the child in disgust at what she had done, and then declared she was still pregnant and would bring the child up as her own.

Meanwhile in another part of the tangled fertility forest, a lesbian couple, Dawn and Lisa, shot to public notoriety. Dawn is four months pregnant, having inseminated herself with sperm from a friend to provide a sibling for Lisa's six-month old daughter, who was conceived from sperm donated into a sterilised pickle jar.

Our society, which feels it can pass no judgement on the way these children were conceived, is roused from its moral torpor only when it comes to paying for them. Thus, the Child Support Agency lumbered into action, pursuing one father in a pickle jar and another in a hypodermic syringe for recompense.

What both cases have in common is an extreme reductionism of human identity in which children are no more than the product of randomly assembled parts and fathers a mechanically recovered emission of bodily fluids.

Both dismember procreation to its component parts of sex, conception and pregnancy. Both mean a child is conceived in the absence of a loving, or indeed any emotional, human engagement.

Both turn the child into a commodity, an object to be created or destroyed as a mere instrument of adult happiness. And both have demonstrated once again the way advances in medical technology expose our current moral confusion.

Of course, one cannot fail to sympathise with the plight of the Dutch couple, driven to rent Mrs Roche's womb by the desolation of childlessness. Their tragedy has now been hideously compounded by this appalling mess.

But compassion alone cannot motivate public policy, especially where the risks of doing harm to others are so pronounced. Surrogacy is intensely undesirable and should be actively discouraged. Sometimes it can produce great joy, as we saw recently with the triplets borne by a surrogate on behalf of their ecstatic genetic parents.

But such intended happiness all too often goes disastrously wrong and does terrible harm. There may be conflicts over ownership of the child, as in the case of the Peters family. The intended parents may reject the child because it is handicapped, or they change their minds. Even where the baby is handed over without argument, the surrogate mother is often left deeply depressed, which is hardly surprising. The biological bond formed in pregnancy between the mother and the unborn child is intense and important, however loudly the surrogate may deny it.

No wonder Mrs Roche found she couldn't go through with the abortion. Women are not human warehouses. To treat them as such not only degrades them as women but hits them at a profound level in their psyche.

And then there are the interests of the child, the last person to be considered in these situations. If the Peters family kept the child it would have been rejected by its biological mother and brought up by its natural father and stepmother.

If Mrs Roche kept it, it would be deprived of its natural father who, in any case, played no other role in its conception than inserting a syringe into its mother, who was 'shocked and stunned' by the whole process – for which she was paid. To classify the £12,000 as 'expenses' is a transparent fiction.

What would any of that do to a child's all-important sense of identity? Given these damaging personal and social consequences, how can surrogacy be permitted, paid or not?

The dismemberment of procreation corrupts the essence of family. It's true that adopted children usually manage to overcome these problems of identity, but they still have them. The point is that artificial insemination wilfully creates them.

A child is properly the outcome of a close and loving human contact between the people who created it. Whenever that is interrupted, the child treats it as a rejection by one or both parents, leading to potentially deep problems with identity and self-worth.

This applies to any kind of artificial insemination by donor. The pickle jar pregnancy is but one point on a continuum from AID through in-vitro fertilisation to surrogacy. The issue is not whether lesbians are able to care properly for children – they are as able or unable as anyone else – but rather that the 'right' to have a child has blinded us to the dereliction of duty to act in the most fundamental interests of that child.

There is surely no 'right' to a child. Fertility is a stroke of good fortune. Infertility is a grievous affliction but treating children as commodities is worse, for them and for all of us.

Melanie Phillips, The *Observer*, 18 May 1997

Birth Control

In my opinion as a Feminist and a Communist, the fundamental importance and value of birth control lie in its widening of the scope of human freedom and choice, its self-determining significance for women. For make no mistake about this: Birth Control, the diffusion of the knowledge and possibility of Birth Control, means freedom for women, social and sexual freedom, and that is why it is so intensely feared and disliked in many influential quarters to-day. For thousands of years births and the rearing – and often the losing – of unlimited broods of babies were considered to be women's business *par excellence*. But that women should think about this business, that they should judge and examine it, that they should look at their future and their children's future . . . this is, indeed, camouflage it as you may, the beginning of the end of a social system and a moral code.

Let me develop very briefly and sketchily my assertion that Birth Control means sexual freedom. The ostensible reasons for the established form of patriarchal marriage have always been (a) the inheritance of property, and (b) the protection ensured to the young children and to their mother during her child-bearing period. But when marriage no longer means the subjection of unlimited motherhood and the economic dependence of mothers, the main social reasons for its retention as a stereotyped monogamous formula will be at an end. Observe, I do not say that Birth Control will abolish or diminish real monogamy: there will probably always be as much, or rather as little, monogamy as there has always been. But it will no longer be stereotyped as the one lifelong and unvarying form of legally recognised expression for anything so infinitely variable and individual as the sexual impulse.

Now the demand for Birth Control has long ago ceased to be academic. It is becoming very urgent and more widespread than many persons, even among those interested and sympathetic, quite realise. This demand touches the lives of the majority of women in this and every country very acutely. Any one who knows the lives and work of the wives and mothers of the working class – or, as I, a Communist, would prefer to style it the exploited class –

45

who has helped them and striven to teach them, not in the spirit of a schoolmistress, but as a fellow-woman and a friend – knows that these women are in no doubt as to the essential righteousness of their claim to control their own maternity. But how? Hardly any of these women, if she can speak to you fully and frankly as a friend, but will admit that – often more than once – she has, on finding herself in the hideously significant phrase they use, 'caught,' had recourse either to drugs or to most violent internal operative methods in order to bring about a miscarriage. And these operative methods have, of course, been applied absolutely without antiseptic or aseptic precautions, and without any of the rest which is as essential after such an experiment as after a normal confinement at full term. Yet it ought not to be beyond the powers of medical and chemical science to invent an absolutely reliable contraceptive!

Think of the marvels of destruction in the shape of asphyxiating and corrosive gases all ready for the next great war for liberty and civilisation. Think of the knowledge we have already attained of the structure and functions of the endocrine glands, and the work which has been done in the direction of modifying, renewing or transforming sexuality and procreative power . . . Surely a science which can perform such wonders, though the technique is obviously only in its first stages, should be able to prevent conception without injuring health or impairing natural pleasure! . . .

Now I am not concerned here to vindicate the moral right to abortion, though I am profoundly convinced that it is a woman's right, and have argued the case for that right in the Press, both in England and America. I am told, however, by one of the leaders of our movement, to whose penetrating judgement and wide nursing experience I give the highest honour, that abortion is physiologically dangerous and to be deprecated. It is open, perhaps, to question whether the effects of abortion itself have been sufficiently separated from the appalling bad conditions of nervous terror, lack of rest and lack of surgical cleanliness in which it is generally performed. But granted that it is injurious *per se*, the demand for effective contraception is all the stronger. The ancient codes, the decaying superstitions and prejudices of an old theoretical morality which has never been thoroughly accepted in practice, are losing all the sanctity they ever had. For an increasing number of persons throughout the world, including all the most mentally capable and physically vigorous, they mean just nothing at all.

It is up to science to meet the demands of humanity; and one of the most urgent of those demands is that of true eugenics (not privilege and property defence) that shall be given as Anna Wickham says, 'frankly, gaily,' or – not at all. Which shall it be?

F. W. Stella Browne, *The Feminine Aspect of British Culture*, 1922

Frozen Embryos

Yesterday, according to plan, the destruction began of some 3,000 dream children. They were surplus human embryos, produced in fertility clinics, and kept frozen for over five years. Whatever our personal view of the ethical implications of such a process, this is a poignant moment which should give us all pause for reflection. Here was human potential that has never been realised. Cardinal Hume, who has vigorously denounced the whole procedure of creating so many surplus embryos and then destroying them, has nevertheless been quoted as saying in this case, 'they should be disposed of with dignity and it would be appropriate to say a prayer.'

Trying to think of a suitable epitaph for these unborn dream children, I turned to one of the *Essays of Elia*. Charles Lamb, who lived a lonely bachelor life, indulges in day dreams in which he sees the children that might have been, playing in his garden. Then as the vision fades, he writes, 'While I stood gazing, both the children gradually grew fainter in my view, receding and still receding, till nothing at last but two mournful features were seen in the uttermost distance, which, without speech, strangely impressed upon me the effects of speech (as they called) . . .

'We are not children at all; we are nothing; less than nothing, and dreams. We see only what might have been, and must wait upon the tedious shores of Lethe millions of ages before we have existence and a name.'

Those of us who, through no conscious choice of our own, are childless, can identify with that longing for our dream children. There is a sense in which we feel that we too have not realised our full human potential if we have not passed on life to another generation. Yet, this is to take a limited view of what it means to belong to the whole human community. There's an African saying that 'every child is everyone's child'. That is to say that we are all responsible in some way for the nurture of every child God entrusts to human hands. Yet in the same world where yesterday 3,000 embryos were due to be destroyed, some 30,000 real children died as a result of hunger or sickness, poverty or the aftermath of war. They too have their epitaph. Like the smallest of the birds, not one of them falls to the ground, said Jesus without their heavenly Father caring for them. And His promise to them goes far beyond the limits of their short existence here on earth. 'Their angels,' said Jesus, 'continually behold the face of our father in heaven.' So let's pray for all children, born or unborn, those who have existence and a name and those whose very existence has been cut off and whose name is known only to God.

Dr Pauline Webb, BBC *Prayer for the Day*, 2 August 1996

7. War

We do not yet know what will happen in France or whether the French resistance will be prolonged, both in France and in the French Empire overseas. The French government will be throwing away great opportunities and casting adrift their future if they do not continue the war in accordance with their Treaty obligations, from which we have not felt able to release them. The House will have read the historic declaration in which, at the desire of many Frenchmen – and of our own hearts – we have proclaimed our willingness at the darkest hour in French history to conclude a union of common citizenship in this struggle. However matters may go in France or with the French government or other French governments, we in this island and in the British Empire will never lose our sense of comradeship with the French people. If we are now called upon to endure what they have been suffering, we shall emulate their courage, and if final victory rewards our toils they shall share the gains, aye, and freedom shall be restored to all. We abate nothing of our just demands: not one jot or tittle do we recede. Czechs, Poles, Norwegians, Dutch, Belgians have joined their causes to our own. All these shall be restored.

What General Weygand called the Battle of France is over. I expect that the Battle of Britain is about to begin. Upon this battle depends the survival of Christian civilization. Upon it depends our own British life, and the long continuity of our institutions and our empire. The whole fury and might of the enemy must very soon be turned on us. Hitler knows that he will have to break us in this island or lose the war. If we can stand up to him, all Europe may be free and the life of the world may move forward into broad, sunlit uplands. But if we fail, then the whole world, including the United States, including all that we have known and cared for, will sink into the abyss of a new Dark Age made more sinister, and perhaps more protracted, by the lights of perverted science. Let us therefore brace ourselves to our duties and so bear ourselves that, if the British Empire and its Commonwealth last for a thousand years, men will still say, 'This was their finest hour.'

Winston Churchill (1874–1965), BBC broadcast, 18 June 1940

He who uses force unsparingly, without reference to the bloodshed involved, must obtain a superiority if his adversary uses less vigour in its application . . .

To introduce into a philosophy of war principles of moderation would be an absurdity. War is an act of violence pushed to its utmost limits.

Karl von Clausewitz (1770–1831), 'Vom Kriege'/'On War', published 1833, English translation 1873

Modern wars are not made by nations or by peoples, nor are they made by men in a state of aggression welling over with instinct of territory. Wars are usually made by a few individuals in positions of great power, 'great leaders,' 'thoughtful' and 'respected' statesmen generally advised by 'the best and brightest' almost always with calm and deliberation, and the pretence if not conviction of complete moral rectitude. Generals removed far from the battlefront give orders for the annihilation of the 'enemy' with no more aggressiveness or emotion than when they order the gardener at home to mow the lawn a little closer. The 'fighting' man shoots at or drops his bombs on an 'enemy' he hardly ever sees, and from whom his emotional disengagement could scarcely be more remote. He is engaged in 'hostilities' in which there is no emotional enmity, and in 'aggressive' behaviour in which there is no feeling of aggression.

His behaviour is not instinctive but State-directed towards the enemy. Such aggression – legitimized aggression – is justified and legitimized by a collectivity, whether State, political party, a cause, or a self-appointed prophet, and is acted out by individuals for reasons that are self-transcending rather than self-assertive. Neither psychological processes, instincts, nor learning paradigms are involved in such 'aggression', and it is virtually empty of cultural content. Enemies are indicated and the subjects are called upon to demonstrate their loyalty. In war, explained the French biologist Jean Rostand, 'man is much more a sheep than a wolf. He follows, he obeys. War is servility, rather – a certain fanaticism and credulity – but not aggressiveness.' The truth is – and this is perhaps the greatest of all paradoxes – motivationally, war represents one of the least aggressive forms of human behaviour. A state is not a natural creation but an artificial entity, and it is as such artificial entities that states wage war, with artificial weapons from artificial motives for artificial purposes, conducted for artificial ends.

It was the superpatriotism of such militarists as General Friedrich von Bernhard whipped up in his notorious book *Germany and the Next War*, published in 1911, and read throughout the civilised world with fascination and more than a certain grudging admiration, that formulated Germany's program for the First World War. Bernhard, quite evidently an upright and honest man, seemed to have been convinced by his own rectitude that what he believed must therefore be true, and since virtually every German from the Kaiser to the simplest citizen thoroughly agreed with him, there could be no doubt of the truth of his claims. He wrote the book, he declared, to protest against 'the aspiration for peace, which seemed to dominate our age and threaten to poison the soul of the German people.' 'War,' he declared, 'is a biological necessity, as necessary as the struggle of the elements in nature. It gives a biologically just decision, since its decisions rest on the very nature of things.' 'The whole idea' of arbitration 'represents a presumptuous encroachment on natural laws of development,' for 'what is right is decided by the arbitrament of war.'

The idea had an immense appeal, not only for the German militarists but also for their counterparts and industrialists everywhere, just as do the ideas today of Lorenz, Ardrey, Morris, and other innate aggressionists. Perhaps none of these writers subscribe to Bernhard's idea that the arbitrament of war is alone capable of giving the only biologically just decision between nations, but they do agree with the General that the drive towards war is a natural one and that in the past at any rate, it played an adaptively valuable role in human evolution. The evidence, however, seems to indicate that the opposite is true and that in fact war has become increasingly dysgenic and now threatens all life on earth.

Warfare is here as a part of our thoughts; the deeds of warriors are immortalised in the words of our poets, the toys of our children are modelled upon weapons of soldiers, the frames of reference within which politicians and diplomats work always contain war. If we know that it is not inevitable, that it is due to historical accident that warfare is one of the ways in which we think of behaving, are we given any hope by that? What hope is there of persuading nations to abandon war, nations so thoroughly imbued with the idea that to resort to war is, if not actually desirable and noble, at least inevitable whenever certain defined circumstances arise?

In answer to this question we might turn to the history of other inventions which must once have seemed as firmly entrenched as warfare. Take the method of trial which preceded the jury system: ordeal and trial by combat. Unfair, capricious, alien as they are to our feeling today, they were once the only methods open to individuals accused of some offence. The invention of trial by jury gradually replaced these methods until only witches, and finally not even witches, had to resort to the ordeal. The ordeal did not go because people thought it unjust or wrong; it went out of use because a method more congruent with the institutions and feeling of the period was invented. Poor inventions often give way to better ones. For this to happen, two conditions, at least, are necessary. First people must recognise the defects of the old invention, and someone must develop a new one.

'Swimming against the tide', *Peace Pledge Union Book*, 1997

Once more unto the breach, dear friends, once more;
Or close the wall up with our English dead!
In peace there is nothing so becomes a man
as modest stillness and humility:
But when the blast of war blows in our ears,
Then imitate the action of the tiger;
Stiffen the sinews, summon up the blood,
Disguise fair nature with hard-favour'd rage;
Then lend the eye a terrible aspect;
Let it pry through the portage of the head
Like the brass cannon; let the brow o'erwhelm it
As fearfully as doth a galled rock
O'erhang and jutty his confounded base,
Swill'd with the wild and wasteful ocean.
Now set the teeth and stretch the nostril wide;
Hold hard the breath, and bend up every spirit
To his full height! – On, on, you noble English,
Whose blood is fet from fathers of war-proof!
Fathers that, like so many Alexanders,
Have in these parts from morn till even fought,
And sheath'd their swords for lack of argument: –
Dishonour not your mothers; now attest
That those whom you call'd fathers did beget you!
Be copy now to men of grosser blood,
And teach them how to war! – and you, good yeomen,
Whose limbs were made in England, show us here
The mettle of your pasture; let us swear
That you are worth your breeding: which I doubt not;
For there is none of you so mean and base,
That hath not noble lustre in your eyes.
I see you stand like greyhounds in the slips,
Straining upon the start. The game's afoot:
Follow your spirit; and upon this charge
Cry – God for Harry! England! and Saint George!

William Shakespeare (1564–1616), *Henry V* act 3, sc.1

O Lord our God, help us to tear their soldiers to bloody shreds with our shells; help us to cover their smiling fields with the pale forms of their patriot dead; help us to drown the thunder of the guns with the wounded, writhing in pain; help us to lay waste their humble homes with a hurricane of fire; help us to wring the hearts of their unoffending widows with unavailing grief; help us to turn them out roofless with their little children to wander unfriended through wastes of their desolated land in rags and hunger and thirst, sport of the sun-flames of summer and the icy winds of winter, broken in spirit, worn with travail, imploring Thee for the refuge of the grave and denied it – for our sakes, who adore Thee, Lord, blast their hopes, blight their lives, protract their bitter pilgrimage, make heavy their steps, water their way with their tears, stain the white snow with the blood of their wounded feet! We ask of one who is the Spirit of love and who is the ever-faithful refuge and friend of all that are sore beset, and seek His aid with humble and contrite hearts. Grant our prayer, O Lord, and Thine shall be the praise and honor and glory now and ever, Amen.

Mark Twain (1835–1910)

8. *Wildlife*

Human beings treat animals appallingly. We protect landscapes but wipe out the creatures that live in them. We shape our pets to fit our fantasies, the deformities of dogs are a disgrace. Laboratory animals are 'models': biochemistry on legs. But the most wide-spread abuses are in farming, where animals are hustled from birth to slaughter with unalleviated stress along the way – and it's getting worse, as new technologies override their physiology more and more comprehensively. Legislation helps, but the concept that could truly make a difference is that of animal rights.

But people – including politicians and moral philosophers – misunderstand the idea. None of us is born with rights. They are not a property of flesh. We need not suppose that they are 'God given' and it is difficult to argue that they are inalienable. Rights are a convenience, a social device, that makes it easier for us to live with each other. I don't want you to invade my space: take up residence in my house, borrow my socks, send my children on errands. In exchange I agree without demur to treat you and yours with equal grace. You should respect whatever I care about and in exchange I will respect whatever you care about (if there is any clash, we can argue about it).

But it is boring for humans to list all the things they care about every time they encounter each other. It is quicker and easier to include everything that each of us holds to be sacred or important under one blanket term 'rights'. None of us 'possess' rights. But I am willing to pretend that you have rights, provided you adopt the same pretence. Existentialists and relativists might say that whatever we choose to pretend becomes reality, for that is all the reality there is. Or we can admit that 'rights' is a term of convenience. The philosophical superstructure is malleable; but 'rights' remains an unimprovably convenient social device. Once the concept is in place, we need not bother to think about the details.

But should we accord rights only to other humans? Some aboriginal peoples believe that rocks and rivers have rights. Why not? The socially convenient device that protects us from each other can serve to protect our surroundings. The all-embracing concept of rights will help us to respect the things we value, whatever those things might be.

To the broad concept of 'rights', sophisticates have added three conditional clauses: commensurability, responsibility, and sensibility. Fail any one of the three and – no rights. Jolly bad luck, but there you go. Animals seem to fail on at least two counts and, until the last few years, were deemed in most scientific circles to fail in the third as well.

Commensurability in this context means tit for tat. I credit you with 'rights' so long as you respect mine. But suppose you have no power to invade my space? Why should I care? So the notion has arisen that rights are proportional to power; the most powerful are the most able to encroach on others and must be placated accordingly. The rich have more 'rights' than the poor. Animals have no effective power, so it seems silly to grant them 'rights'. But this sounds callous, uncivilised. So we dress it up a little: people earn rights in so far as they have and accept responsibility. Cows and pigs accept no responsibility and certainly not towards us. Therefore they have no rights.

Of course, this argument quickly runs into trouble. Do babies have responsibility? What of people with Alzheimer's, or in a coma? We can get around this with a little pragmatism: we were all babies once, and if babies were not granted rights then none would get to be adults. Any of us might be struck down so we should grant rights to the unfortunate. None of us will be chickens, however, so again, the notion of 'rights' does not apply.

But is it ineluctably the case that rights and responsibilities should go together? This is an arbitrary codicil; as arbitrary as the concept of 'rights' itself. Rights is a device for respect. If we think animals are worthy of respect then we should credit them with rights irrespective of any feelings that they might have for us.

What of sentience? One of the least attractive contributions of science in this century has proved to be that of behaviourism, initiated before World War I in part by Ivan Pavlov but primarily by the American J.B. Watson. The aim was laudable enough – to make animal psychology a true science; and Watson and his colleagues argued, in positivist vein, that nothing can be a science that is not based exclusively on qualities that can be directly observed and quantified. Thoughts and feelings cannot be measured and so were left out of account. All that could actually be measured was behaviour. Hence 'behaviourism'.

Thus stated, the approach was sensible. The behaviourists were acknowledging Sir Peter Medawar's adage – that 'science is the art of the soluble'. Ask questions about behaviour, and they could be answered. Ask about the goings-on in an animal's head, and you were reduced to arm waving. Ergo, stick to behaviour. In effect, the behaviourists regarded animals as if they were machines, like alarm clocks. The alarm clock (metaphorically speaking) became the 'model' to which animals were compared.

However, most of the behaviourists and their followers then made a huge mistake. It was fair enough to leave thoughts and feelings out of account as an experimental convenience, it does not make sense to begin with what is simple and measurable, and expand the horizons if and when this proves necessary. But the behaviourists forgot that the alarm clock was a model. Soon they were arguing effectively as a matter of dogma that animals are machines. Any suggestion that they think, or can be conscious, or feel or indeed can be stressed (except in so far as a machine can be 'stressed' by wear and tear) was ridiculed. The suggestion that a mother seal feels grief when her pup is battered to death before her eyes was dismissed as sentimental 'anthropomorphism': ascribing human attributes to non-humans. However human their moans and anxiety might seem, the dogma said the seals were machines, and therefore felt nothing. A chicken might look distressed when rammed in a small wire box with three others, but that was an illusion. Chickens are machines. Only their behaviour is measurable.

In practice, observations of animals throughout this century have defied behaviourist interpretation. The wild chimpanzees that Jane Goodall observed in the sixties cannot sensibly be compared to any machine; and over the past few decades the study first of animals' thinking and then of their emotions have again become respectable. Accordingly, the old spectre of anthropomorphism has taken a new turn. Since the alarm-clock model of animals has proved inadequate, psychologists need a new model, and the human being is not a bad point of comparison since we are appropriately complex and yet we do have a privileged insight into our own psychology.

So all in all, respectable science has now caught up with the animal-lovers, now it is clearly perverse not to perceive animals as sentient beings, who register their emotional responses with varying degrees of consciousness. It seems impossible to know precisely what animals feel, but impossible to deny that they do feel. This does not mean that we have to grant them rights, but the last traditional excuse for denying them rights is gone. No one sensible can support the view that a pig or a cow is not sentient. But if we do acknowledge that animals have rights, how should we treat them?

There are various answers, all with an arbitrary feel because that is the nature of moral philosophy. One is that our prime responsibility should be to our own species no matter how much respect we accord to others. This is arguable but reasonable, and other animals would surely feel the same if they could discuss the matter. Our physiology is such that we cannot easily survive as out-and-out vegans – not unless we have access to a health-food shop and can afford its refinements. We do not need much meat but we tend to languish if we don't have any, or milk, fish and eggs. The vegetarian argument that we could feed many more people if we did not raise livestock for meat, is true only up to a point. It is profligate to do as the Western world does, and feed at least half of the home-grown grain to livestock. Yet an agriculture based entirely on plants would be less productive than one which included animals as well. The Indian sacred cow looks like a terrible waste, and in some circumstances might be, but it thrives on rubbish and produces calves in passing, and without the oxen that those calves become, village India would come to a stop. It would, in short, be hugely irresponsible to advocate universal veganism. So it is not an option to abandon livestock altogether and the moral challenge is to raise farm animals, but to respect them. The point is to keep them in ways that let them to do things, physical and social, they would do in the wild and to slaughter them as untraumatically as possible.

In conservation the moral principle is that of *noblesse oblige*. Humans have messed up the world so much that other animals – what is left of them – cannot survive unless we now take their affairs in hand. The best that we do for creatures is provide national parks, but these are rarely adequate. Third World national parks commonly contain more domestic cattle than wildlife. Britain's are overwhelmingly in uplands where intensive agriculture is too difficult, and, outside Alaska, even the biggest in the US – Yellowstone – is probably too small for grizzly bears. Unless we supplement the wild populations by captive breeding and cull those populations that out-grow their reserves, then over the next century we can say goodbye to most of the world's largest terrestrial mammals.

Is it possible, though, to raise farm animals humanely? In practice, common sense is not a bad guide to husbandry. It is obviously not kind to keep a pig up to its belly in freezing mud, as often happened in the past, but not kind either to keep a sow in an iron crate where she can barely stand and lie, let alone turn round, while her piglets suckle through the bars. It is perverse to suggest that four hens in a wire cage, their eyes dilated in what looks very like fear, their bones so weakened by too much laying that they break if the bird is handled, are enjoying life. We could not suppose that this was acceptable unless we were either indifferent, or gulled into the behaviourist belief that an animal is a machine and machines cannot feel.

Yet we should not be casually anthropomorphic. We should not assume that whatever pleases us would also please a chicken or a pig. If we want to devise husbandry that is truly kind, then we should try to understand what each kind of creature wants. In the Eighties at Edinburgh University, the late David Woodgush adopted an *ethological* approach; attempting to base the husbandry of pigs upon their behaviour in the wild. He gave them *carte blanche* in a variety of environments and effectively incited them to demonstrate what it is they like to do, and found, for example, – that sows, given the chance, build nests out of straw for their offspring; that if they are not stressed they do not lie on them and crush them; and that unstressed boars can be left with the sow and piglets. His successors are trying to find out how important each item of natural behaviour is to the animal. Thus at Oxford University Dr Marian Stamp Dawkins seeks to quantify the effort that hens are prepared to make to achieve particular goals. She has found they will work hard to find their way to a nest-box to lay eggs.

But wouldn't it be ridiculously expensive to allow sows and hens to build their own nests? There are many answers to this. First humane and more relaxed husbandry is dearer than the factory kind, but not outlandishly so. In principle, too, humane husbandry can be combined with other pursuits; pigs are woodland animals, for example, and were traditionally raised in forests, so there was no need to build expensive pens. If humane husbandry was universal, we would produce less meat and eggs than now – but nutritionally and gastronomically, that would be a good thing. Westerners eat more meat and dairy products than are good for us and the fundamental reason is not that we have an innate desire to do so (we are omnivores, not carnivores) but that agriculture is most profitable when it produces lots of livestock (livestock is the key to value-adding), and to some degree we have become compliant consumers.

The final argument – that meat should be cheap so that poor people can afford it – is the last recourse of scoundrels, hypocrisy at its most flagrant. In truth, meat should be expensive. It is ludicrous to pay less than £5 a pound for turkey. It is sold at giveaway prices only because the birds are raised under conditions of extreme hideousness. If people cannot afford expensive meat it is because our economy is designed to ensure that some people are extremely poor, while others are ridiculously rich. Cheap meat serves the same purposes in our own gruesome society as bread and circuses in ancient Rome: a sop to the masses. Again it is a matter of pecking order. The poor stay poor so that the rich can be rich, but beneath the poor are the animals, who make their lot tolerable.

Farm animals, in short, are the fall-guys, who make it possible to sustain inequity. These two massive wrongs do not make a right.

Colin Tudge, Visiting Research Fellow, Centre for Philosophy, London School of Economics, *Independent on Sunday*, 16 March 1997

Part 2 The Way We Are

9. Age and Ageing

All the world's a stage,
And all the men and women merely players;
And one man in his time plays many parts,
His acts being seven ages. At first, the infant,
Mewling and puking in the nurse's arms.
Then the whining schoolboy, with his satchel
And shining morning face, creeping like snail
Unwillingly to school. And then the lover,
Sighing like furnace, with a woeful ballad
Made to his mistress' eyebrow. Then a soldier,
Full of strange oaths and bearded like the pard,
Jealous in honour, sudden and quick in quarrel,
Seeking the bubble reputation
Even in the cannon's mouth. And then the justice,
In fair round belly with good capon lined,
With eyes severe and beard of formal cut,
Full of wise saws and modern instances;
And so he plays his part. The sixth age shifts
Into lean and slippered pantaloon,
With spectacles on nose and pouch on side;
His youthful hose, well saved, a world too wide
for his shrunk shank, and his big manly voice,
Turning again toward childish treble, pipes
And whistles in his sound. Last of all,
Is second childishness and mere oblivion,
Sans teeth, sans eyes, sans taste, sans everything.

William Shakespeare (1564–1616), 'The Seven Ages', *As You Like It*

How foolish to think one can ever slam the door in the face of age. Much wiser to be polite and gracious and ask him to lunch in advance.

Noel Coward (1899–1973), Diary, 3 June 1956

Now I find I grow old, my sight is decayed, so that I cannot read a small print, unless in a strong light. My strength is decayed, so that I walk much slower than I did some years since. My memory of names, whether of persons or places, is decayed, till I stop a little to recollect them.

What I should be afraid of is, if I took thought for the morrow, that my body should weigh down my mind, and create either stubbornness, by the decrease of my understanding, or peevishness, by the increase of bodily infirmities.

John Wesley, 28th June 1789, his eighty-sixth birthday.

At a dinner to celebrate the seventieth birthday of Mark Twain, William Dean Howells proposed a toast in which he said, 'in wishing the health of our honoured and, in view of his great age, revered guest, I will not say, "O King, Live forever!" but "O King, live as long as you like!"' There was much laughter and applause as Mark Twain rose to reply.

Well, if I had made that joke it would be the best one I ever made, and in the prettiest language, too. I never can get quite to that height. But I appreciate that joke, and I shall remember it – and I shall use it when occasion requires.

I have had a great many birthdays in my time. I remember the first one very well, and I always think of it with indignation: everything was so crude, unaesthetic, primeval. Nothing like this at all. No proper appreciative preparation made; nothing neatly ready. Now, for a person born with high and delicate instincts – why, even the cradle wasn't whitewashed – nothing ready at all. I hadn't my hair, I hadn't my teeth, I hadn't any clothes, I had to go to my first banquet just like that. Well, everybody came swarming in. It was the merest little bit of a village – hardly that, just a little hamlet, in the backwoods of Missouri, where nothing ever happened, and the people were all interested, and they all came: they looked me over to see if there was anything fresh in my line. Why, nothing ever happened in that village. I, – Why, I was the only thing that had really happened there for months and months and months: and although I say it myself that shouldn't, I came the nearest to being a real event that had happened in that village in more than two years. Well, those people came, they came with that curiosity which is so provincial, with that frankness which also is so provincial, and they examined me all around and gave their opinion. Nobody asked them and I shouldn't have minded if anyone had paid me a compliment, but nobody did. Their opinions were all just green with prejudice, and I feel those opinions to this day. Well, I stood that as long as – you know I was courteous, and I stood it to the limit. I stood it an hour, and then the worm turned. I was the worm; it was my turn to turn, and I turned. I knew very well the strength of my position; I knew that I was the only spotlessly pure and innocent person in that whole town, and I came out and said so. And they could not say a word. It was so true. They blushed: they were embarrassed. Well, that was the first after-dinner speech I ever made. I think it was after dinner.

It's a long stretch between that first birthday speech and this one. That was my cradle song, and this is my swan song, I suppose. I am used to swan songs: I have sung them several times.

This is my seventieth birthday, and I wonder if you all rise to the size of that proposition, realizing all the significance of that phrase, seventieth birthday.

The seventieth birthday! It is the time of life when you arrive at a new and awful dignity: when you may throw aside the decent reserves which have oppressed you for a generation and stand unafraid and unabashed upon your seven-terraced summit and look down and teach – unrebuked. You can tell the world how you got there. It is what they all do. You shall never get tired of telling by what delicate arts and deep moralities you climb up to that great place. You will explain the process and dwell on the particulars with senile rapture. I have been anxious to explain my own system this long time, and now at last I have the right.

I have achieved my seventy years in the usual way: by sticking strictly to a scheme of life which would kill anybody else. It sounds like an exaggeration, but that is really the common rule for attaining old age. When we examine the programme of any of these garrulous old people we always find that the habits which have preserved them would have decayed us: that the way of life which enabled them to live upon the property of their heirs so long, as Mr. Choate says, would have put us out of commission ahead of time. I will offer here, as a sound maxim, this: that we can't reach old age by another man's road.

I will now teach, offering my way of life to whomsoever desires to commit suicide by the scheme which has enabled me to beat the doctor and the hangman for seventy years. Some of the details may sound untrue, but they are not. I am not here to deceive. I am here to teach.

We have no permanent habits until we are forty. Then they begin to harden, presently they petrify, then business begins. Since forty I have been regular about going to bed and getting up – and that is one of the main things. I have made it a rule to go to bed when there wasn't anybody left to sit up with: and I have made it a rule to get up when I had to. This has resulted in an unswerving regularity of irregularity. It has saved me sound, but it would injure another person.

In the matter of diet – which is another main thing – I have been persistently strict in sticking to the things which didn't agree with me until one or the other of us got the best of it. Until lately I got the best of it myself. But last spring I stopped frolicking with mince pie after midnight: up to then I had always believed it wasn't loaded. For thirty years I have taken coffee and bread at eight in the morning, and no bite nor sup until seven-thirty in the evening. Eleven hours. That is all right for me, and is wholesome, because I have never had a headache in my life, but headachy people would not reach seventy comfortably by that road, and they would be foolish to try it. And I wish to urge upon you this – which I think is wisdom – that if you find that you can't make seventy by any but an uncomfortable road, don't you go. When they take you off the Pullman and retire you to the rancid smoker, put on your things, count your checks, and get out at the first way station where there's a cemetery.

I have made it a rule never to smoke more than one cigar at a time. I have no other restriction as regards smoking. I do not know just when I began to smoke, I only know it was in my father's lifetime, and that I was discreet. He passed from this life early in 1847, when I was a shade past eleven: ever since then I have smoked publicly. As an example to others, and not that I care for moderation myself, it has always been my rule never to smoke when asleep, and never to refrain when awake. It is a good rule. I mean, for me: but some of you know quite well that it wouldn't answer for everybody that's trying to get to be seventy.

I smoke in bed until I have to go to sleep: I wake up in the night, sometimes once, sometimes twice, sometimes three times, and I never waste any of these opportunities to smoke. This habit is so old and dear and precious to me that I would feel as you, sir, would feel if you should lose the only moral you've got – meaning the chairman – if you've got one: I am making no charges. I will grant, here, that I have stopped smoking now and then, for a few months at a time, but it was not on principle, it was only to show off: it was to pulverize those critics who said I was a slave to my habits and couldn't break my bonds. To-day it is all of sixty years since I began to smoke the limit. I have never bought cigars with life bands around them. I early found that those were too expensive for me. I have always bought cheap cigars – reasonably cheap, at any rate. Sixty years ago they cost me four dollars a barrel, but my taste has improved, latterly, and I pay seven now. Six or seven. Seven, I think. Yes. It's seven but that includes the barrel. I often have smoking parties at my house: but the people that come have always just taken the pledge. I wonder why that is?

As for drinking I have no rule about that. When the others drink, I like to help: otherwise I remain dry, by habit and pre-ference. This dryness does not hurt me, but it could easily hurt you, because you are different. You let it alone.

Since I was seven years old I have seldom taken a dose of medicine, and have still seldomer needed one. But up to seven I lived exclusively on allopathic medicines. Not that I needed them, for I don't think I did: it was for economy: my father took a drug store for a debt, and it made cod-liver oil cheaper than the other breakfast foods. We had nine barrels of it, and it lasted me seven years. Then I was weaned. The rest of the family had to get along with rhubarb and ipecac and such things, because I was the pet. I was the first Standard Oil Trust. I had it all. By the time the drug store was exhausted my health was established and there has never been much the matter with me since. But you know very well it would be foolish for the average child to start for seventy on that basis. It happened to be just the thing for me, but that was merely an accident: it couldn't happen again in a century.

I have never taken any exercise, except sleeping and resting, and I never intend to take any. Exercise is loathsome. And it cannot be any benefit when you are tired: and I was always tired. But let another person try my way, and see whence he will come out.

I desire now to repeat and emphasize that maxim: We can't reach old age by another man's road. My habits protect my life, but they would assassinate you.

I have lived a severely moral life. But it would be a mistake for other people to try that, or for me to recommend it. Very few would succeed: you have to have a perfectly colossal stock of morals: and you can't get them on a margin: you have to have the whole thing, and put them in your box. Morals are an acquirement – like music, like a foreign language, like piety, poker, paralysis – no man is born with them. I wasn't myself, I started poor. I hadn't a single moral. There is hardly a man in this house that is poorer than I was then. Yes, I started like that – the world before me, not a moral in the slot. Not even an insurance moral. I can remember the first one I ever got. I can remember the landscape, the weather, the – I can remember how everything looked. It was an old moral, an old second-hand moral, all out of repair, and didn't fit, anyway. But if you are careful with a thing like that, and keep it in a dry place, and save it for processions, and Chautauquas, and World's Fairs, and so on, and disinfect it now and then and give it a fresh coat of whitewash once in a while, you will be surprised to see how well she will last and how long she will keep sweet, or at least inoffensive. When I got that mouldy old moral, she had stopped growing, because she hadn't any exercise but I worked her hard, I worked her Sundays and all. Under this cultivation she waxed in might and stature beyond belief, and served me well and was my pride and joy for sixty-three years: then she got to associating with insurance presidents and lost flesh and character, and was a sorrow to look at and no longer competent for business.

She was a great loss to me. Yet not all loss. I sold her – ah, pathetic skeleton, as she was – I sold her to Leopold, the pirate king of Belgium: he sold her to our Metropolitan Museum, and it was very glad to get her, for without a rag on, she stands at 57 feet long and 16 feet high and they think she's a brontosaur. Well, she looks it. They believe it will take nineteen geological periods to breed her match.

Morals are of inestimable value, for every man is born crammed with sin microbes, and the only thing that can extirpate these sin microbes is morals. Now you take a sterilized Christian – I mean, you take *the* sterilized Christian, for there's only one. Dear sir. I wish you wouldn't look at me like that.

Threescore years and ten!

It is the Scriptural statute of limitations. After that, you owe no active duties: for you the strenuous life is over. You are a time-expired man, to use Kipling's military phrase: You have served your term well or less well and you are mustered out. You are become an honorary member of the republic, you are emancipated, compulsions are not for you, nor any bugle call but 'lights out.' You pay the time-worn duty bills if you choose, or decline if you prefer – and without prejudice – for they are not legally collectable.

The previous-engagement plea, which in forty years has cost you so many twinges, you can lay aside forever; on this side of the grave you will never need it again. If you shrink at thought of night, and winter, and the late home-coming from the banquet and the lights and the laughter through the deserted streets – a desolation which would not remind you now, as for a generation it did, that your friends are sleeping, and you must creep in a-tiptoe and not disturb them, but would only remind you that you need not tiptoe, you can never disturb them more – If you shrink at thought of these things, you need only reply, 'Your invitation honours me, and pleases me because you still keep me in your remembrance, but I am seventy; seventy, and would nestle in the chimney corner, and smoke my pipe, and read my book, and take my rest, wishing you well in all affection, and that when you in

71

your turn shall arrive at pier No. 70 you may step aboard your waiting ship with a reconciled spirit, and lay your course toward the sinking sun with a contented heart.'

Mark Twain (1835–1910), Address given at a dinner in New York
on 5 December 1905

> At forty I lost my illusions,
> At fifty I lost my hair,
> At sixty my hope and teeth were gone,
> And my feet were beyond repair.
> At eighty life has clipped my claws,
> I'm bent and bowed and cracked;
> But I can't give up the ghost because
> My follies are intact.

E. Y. Harburg (1898–1981), *Gerontology or Springtime for Senility*

10. Anger

Anybody can become angry – that's easy; but to become angry with the right person, and to the right degree, and at the right time, and for the right purpose, and in the right way – that is not within everybody's power and is not easy.

Aristotle (384–322 BC)

When I am angry I can write, pray, and preach well, for then my whole temperament is quickened, my understanding sharpened, and all mundane vexations and temptations depart.

Martin Luther (1483–1586)

11. Anxiety

Do not look forward to what may happen tomorrow; the same everlasting father, who cares for you today, will take care of you tomorrow, and every day. Either he will shield you from suffering or he will give you unfailing strength to bear it.

St Francis de Sales (1567–1622)

Man, like the bridge, was designed to carry the load of the moment, not the combined weight of a year at once.

William Arthur Ward (1812–82)

12. Death

A corpse is something like the cover of an old book, its contents torn out, and stripped of its lettering and gilding . . . yet the work itself shall not be lost, for it will appear once more in a new and more beautiful edition.

Benjamin Franklin (1706–90)

All mankind is of one Author, and is one volume; when one man dies, one chapter is not torn out of the book, but translated into a better language, and every chapter must be so translated; God employs several translators, some pieces are translated by age, some by sickness, some by war, some by justice; but God's hand is in every translation, and his hand shall bind up all our scattered leaves again for that library where every book shall lie open to one another.

John Donne (1572–1631)

A single death is a tragedy, a million deaths is a statistic.

Joseph Stalin (1879–1953)

Death be not proud, though some have called thee
mighty and dreadful, for thou art not so,
For, those, whom thou think'st, thou dost overthrow,
Die not, poor death, nor yet canst thou kill me;
From rest and sleep, which but thy pictures be,
Much pleasure, then from thee, much more must flow,

Here I Stand

And soonest our best men with thee do go,
Rest of their bones, and soul's delivery.
Thou art slave to fate, chance, kings, and desperate men,
And dost with poison, war, and sickness dwell,
And poppy, or charms can make us sleep as well,
And better than thy stroke; why swell'st thou then?
One short sleep past, we wake eternally,
And death shall be no more, Death thou shalt die.

John Donne (1572–1631)

Fidele

Fear no more the heat o' the sun
Nor the furious winter's rages;
Thou thy wordly task hast done,
Home art gone and ta'en thy wages:
Golden lads and girls all must,
As chimney-sweepers, come to dust.

Fear no more the frown o' the great,
Thou art past the tyrant's stroke;
Care no more to clothe and eat;
To thee the reed is as the oak:
The sceptre, learning, physic, must
All follow this, and come to dust.

Fear no more the lightning-flash
Nor the all-dreaded thunder-stone;
Fear not slander, censure rash;
Thou hast finish'd joy and moan:
All lovers young, all lovers must
Consign to thee, and come to dust.

William Shakespeare (1564–1616), *Cymbeline* act 4, sc. 2

Death is nothing at all.
I have only slipped away into the next room.
I am I, and you are you;
whatever we were to each other, that are we still.
Call me by my old familiar name;
speak to me in the easy way you always used;
put no difference into your tone;
wear no forced air of solemnity or sorrow.
Laugh as we always laughed at the little jokes we enjoyed together.
Play – smile – think of me – pray for me.
Let my name be ever the household word that it always was.
Let it be spoken without effect,
without the ghost of a shadow on it.
Life means all that it ever meant;
it is the same as it ever was.
There is absolutely unbroken continuity.

What is this death but negligible accident?
Why should I be out of mind because I am out of sight?
I'm just waiting for you, for an interval,
somewhere very near, just around the corner.
All is well.

Canon Henry Scott Holland, (Words left when he died in 1918)

Do not go gentle into that good night,
Old age should burn and rave at close of day;
Rage, rage against the dying of the light.

Though wise men at their end know dark is right,
Because their words had forked no lightning they
Do not go gentle into that good night.

Good men, the last wave by, crying how bright
Their frail deeds might have danced in a green bay,
Rage, rage against the dying of the light.

Here I Stand

Wild men who caught and sang the sun in flight,
And learn, too late, they grieved it on its way,
Do not go gentle into that good night.

Grave men, near death, who see with blinding sight
Blind eyes could blaze like meteors and be gay,
Rage, rage against the dying of the light.

And you, my father, there on the sad height,
Curse, bless, me now with your fierce tears, I pray.
Do not go gentle into that good night.
Rage, rage against the dying of the light.

Dylan Thomas (1914–53)

13. Evil

The only thing necessary for evil to triumph is for good men to do nothing.

Edmund Burke (1729–97)

Many have puzzled themselves about the origin of evil. I am content to observe that there is evil. And that there is a way to escape from it, and with this I begin and end.

John Newton (1725–1807)

No man chooses evil because it is evil; he only mistakes it for happiness, the good he seeks.

Mary Woolstonecraft (1759–97)

Lady Macbeth speaks:

> The raven himself is hoarse
> That croaks the fatal entrance of Duncan
> Under my battlements. Come, you spirits
> That tend on mortal thoughts, unsex me here,
> fill me, from the crown to the toe, top-full
> of direst cruelty! Make thick my blood,
> Stop up th' access and passage to remorse,
> That no compunctious visitings of nature
> Shake my fell purpose, nor keep peace between
> Th' effect and it! Come to my woman's breasts,

Here I Stand

And take my milk for gall, you murd'ring ministers,
Wherever in your sightless substances
You wait on nature's mischief! Come, thick night,
And pall thee in the dunnest smoke of hell,
That my keen knife see not the wound it makes,
Nor heaven peep through the blanket of the dark,
to cry 'Hold, hold!'

William Shakespeare (1564–1616), Macbeth act 1, sc. 6

14. Friends and Friendship

The most agreeable of all companions is a simple, frank person, without any high pretensions to an oppressive greatness – one who loves life and understands the use of it; obliging alike at all hours; above all, of a golden temper, and steadfast as an anchor. For such an one we gladly exchange the greatest genius, the most brilliant wit, the profoundest thinker.

Gotthold Ephraim Lessing (1729–81)

He who has many friends, has none.

Aristotle (384–322 BC)

The only way to have a friend is be one.

Ralph Waldo Emerson (1803–82)

Friendship ought never to conceal what it thinks.

St Jerome (c. 374–420)

I have often thought, that as longevity is generally desired, and, I believe, generally expected, it would be wise to be continually adding to the number of our friends, that the loss of some may be supplied by others. Friendship, 'the wine of life,' should, like a well-stocked cellar, be thus continually renewed; and it is consolatory to think, that although we can seldom add what will equal the generous first-growths of our youth, yet friendship becomes insensibly old in much less time than is commonly imagined, and not many years are required to make it very mellow and pleasant. Warmth will no doubt, make a considerable difference. Men of affectionate temper and bright fancy will coalesce a great deal sooner than those who are cold and dull.

The proposition which I have now endeavoured to illustrate was, at a subsequent period of his life, the opinion of Johnson himself. He said to Sir Joshua Reynolds, 'If a man does not make new acquaintances as he advances through life, he will soon find himself left alone. A man, Sir, should keep his friendship in constant repair.'

James Boswell (1740–95), *The Life of Samuel Johnson*

It is best to be with those in time we hope to be with in eternity.

Sir Thomas Fuller (1608–61)

When, in disgrace with fortune and men's eyes,
I all alone beweep my outcast state,
And trouble deaf heaven with my bootless cries,
And look upon myself, and curse my fate,
Wishing me like to one more rich in hope,
Featured like him, like him with friends possess'd,
Desiring this man's art and that man's scope,
With what I most enjoy contented least;
Yet in these thoughts myself almost despising,
Haply I think on thee, and then my state,
Like to the lark at break of day arising
From sullen earth, sings hymns at heaven's gate;
For thy sweet love remember'd such wealth brings
That then I scorn to change my state with kings.

William Shakespeare (1564–1616)

Oh, the comfort, the inexpressible comfort of feeling safe with a person, having neither to weigh thoughts nor measure words, but pouring them all right out, just as they are, chaff and grain together; certain that a faithful hand will take and sift them, keep what is worth keeping, and then with the breath of kindness blow the rest away.

Diana Maria Mulock Craik (1826–87)

When to the sessions of sweet silent thought
I summon up remembrance of things past,
I sigh the lack of many a thing I sought,
And with old woes new wail my dear time's waste:
Then can I drown an eye, unused to flow,
For precious friends hid in death's dateless night,
And weep afresh love's long since cancel'd woe,
And moan the expense of many a vanish'd sight:
Then can I grieve at grievances foregone,
And heavily from woe to woe tell o'er
The sad account of fore-bemoaned moan,
Which I new pay as if not paid before.
But if the while I think on thee, dear friend,
All losses are restored and sorrows end.

William Shakespeare (1564–1616)

15. Guilt

From the body of one guilty deed
a thousand ghostly fears and haunting thoughts proceed.

William Wordsworth (1770–1850)

Keep clear of concealment, keep clear of the need of concealment. It is an awful hour when the first necessity of hiding anything comes. The whole life is different thenceforth. When there are questions to be feared and eyes to be avoided and subjects that must not be touched, then the bloom of life is gone.

Phillips Brooks (1835–93)

Whoever profits by the crime is guilty of it.

French Proverb

16. Humanity

No man is an island, entire of itself:
every man is a piece of the continent, a part of the main;
if a clod be washed away by the sea,
Europe is the less, as well as if a promontory were,
as well as if a manor of thy friends or of thine own were;
any man's death diminishes me, because I am involved in mankind;
And therefore never send to know for whom the bell tolls;
It tolls for thee.

John Donne (1572–1631), 'Meditations XVII'

17. Humbug

Upon a careful consideration of my undertaking to give an account of the 'Humbugs of the World' I find myself somewhat puzzled in regard to the true definition of the word. To be sure Webster says that 'humbug' as a noun is an 'imposition under fair pretenses'; and as a verb it is 'to deceive; to impose on.' With all due deference to Dr. Webster I submit that according to present usage this is not the only nor even the generally accepted definition of that term . . . As generally understood 'humbug' consists in putting on glittering appearances – outside show – novel expedients, by which to suddenly arrest public attention, and attract the public eye and ear.

Clergymen, lawyers, or Physicians who should resort to such methods of attracting the Public would not for obvious reasons be apt to succeed. Bankers insurance agents and others who aspire to become custodians of the money of their fellow men would require a different species of advertising from this; but there are various trades and occupations which need only notoriety to insure success, always provided that when customers are once attracted, they never fail to get their money's worth. An honest man who thus arrests public attention will be called a 'humbug' but he is not a swindler or an impostor . . .

When the great blacking-maker of London dispatched his agent to Egypt to write on the pyramids of Ghiza in huge letters:

'Buy Warren's Blacking, 30 Strand, London.'

he was not 'cheating' travellers upon the Nile. His blacking was really a superior article and well worth the price charged for it, but he was 'humbugging' the Public by this queer way of arresting attention. It turned out just as he anticipated, that English travellers in that part of Egypt were indignant at this desecration and they wrote back to the *London Times* (every Englishman writes or threatens to 'write to the *Times*' if anything goes wrong) denouncing the 'Goth' who had thus disfigured these ancient pyramids by writing on them in monstrous letters: 'Buy Warren's Blacking, 30 Strand London.' The *Times* published these letters, and backed them up by several of those awful, grand, and dictatorial editorials peculiar to the greater 'Thunderer' in which the blacking-maker 'Warren, 30 Strand' was stigmatised as a man who had no respect for the ancient patriarchs and it was hinted that he would probably not hesitate to sell his blacking on the sarcophagus of Pharaoh 'or any other' mummy if he could only make money by it. In fact to cap the climax, Warren was denounced as a 'humbug.' These indignant articles were copied into all the provincial journals and very soon, in this manner, the columns of every newspaper in Great Britain were teeming with this advice: 'Try Warren's Blacking, 30 Strand, London.' The curiosity of the public was thus aroused and they did 'try' it, and finding it a superior article they continued to purchase it and recommend it to their friends and Warren made a fortune by it. He always attributed his success to his having 'humbugged' the public by this unique method of advertising his blacking in Egypt! But Warren did not cheat his customers nor practice 'an imposition under fair pretenses.' He was a humbug, but he was an honest upright man and no one called him an impostor or a cheat.

P. T. Barnum (1810–91)

18. Life

To-morrow, and to-morrow, and to-morrow,
Creeps in this petty pace from day to day,
To the last syllable of recorded time;
And all our yesterdays have lighted fools
The way to dusty death. Out, out, brief candle!
Life's but a walking shadow; a poor player,
That struts and frets his hour upon the stage,
And then is heard no more: it is a tale
Told by an idiot, full of sound and fury,
Signifying nothing.

William Shakespeare (1564–1616), *Macbeth* act 5, sc. 5

19. Love

'Mightn't there be something higher than happiness?' he said quietly.

'For example?' Shubin asked and waited.

'Well, for example, you and I, as you say, we're young and sound, let us suppose: each wants happiness for himself . . . But this "happiness" is it the sort of word to unite us, to fire us, to compel us to join hands in friendship? Isn't it a selfish word, I mean a word that keeps people apart?'

'And do you know any words that unite?'

'Yes; and they are not rare either; you know them too.'

'Well, what are they?'

'Well, art, at any rate – since you are an artist – then motherland, science, freedom, justice.'

'And love?' Shubin asked.

'Love unites also – but not the love you are thirsting for now: not love the pleasure, but love the sacrifice.' Shubin frowned.

'That's all right for the Germans: but I want love for myself: I want to be number one.'

'Number one,' Bersyenev repeated. 'Whereas I feel that one's whole destiny in life should be to make oneself number two.'

'If everyone behaved as you recommend,' Shubin said, pulling a face in protest, 'there'd be no one at all to eat the pine-apples – everyone would leave them for someone else.'

'That merely means that pine-apples are not necessities;

89

however, you needn't worry – there will always be people glad to take even the bread out of other people's mouths.'

Ivan Turgenev (1818–83), *On the Eve*

'Loving humility is a terrible force'

At some ideas you stand perplexed, especially at the sight of men's sins, asking yourself whether to combat it by force or by humble love. Always decide: 'I will combat it by humble love.' If you make up your mind about that once and for all, you may be able to conquer the whole world. Loving humility is a terrible force, the strongest of all, and there is nothing like it . . .

Fyodor Dostoevsky (1821–81), *The Brothers Karamazov*

If I speak in the tongues of men and of angels, but have not love, I am a noisy gong or a clanging cymbal. And if I have prophetic powers, and understand all mysteries and all knowledge, and if I have all faith, so as to remove mountains, but have not love, I am nothing. If I give away all that I have, and if I deliver my body to be burned, but have not love, I gain nothing.

Love is patient and kind; love is not jealous or boastful; it is not arrogant or rude. Love does not insist on its own way; it is not irritable or resentful; it does not rejoice at wrong, but rejoices in the right. Love bears all things, believes all things, hopes all things, endures all things.

Love never ends . . . so faith, hope, love abide, these three; but the greatest of these is love.

St Paul, 1 Corinthians 13 (RSV)

20. Marriage

Marriage helps to prevent suicide. Marriage is a prophylactic against depression. It stops excessive drinking. Marriage – deep breath – makes people happier. Those are the stripped-down findings of a market research study we reported yesterday.

Of course, they are generalisations. They speak to the institution of marriage, not to any specific union. Yes, market researchers are more anxious to find out the future demand for pizzas than to plumb psychological depths. But to commercial findings such as this needs to be added a growing mound of high-quality academic work. Stein Ringen, professor of sociology at Oxford, is about to publish a quantitative study showing how marriage makes people richer. Distinguished social researchers, from Ulrich Beck in Munich to Martin Richards in Cambridge, are persuasively arguing the universality of our urge to ensconce mutual love in a permanent bond, and to demonstrate how much better we are for it.

Isn't it curious? Merely to talk in this way sounds ominously like taking a forward position in the current bull market in morality. But it's not that: it actually only registers a profound social fact, albeit one submerged beneath an ocean of 'culture' which fetishises the single state. It is possible to make the case for marriage without adopting the apocalyptic tone of those who read the divorce statistics as if they presaged a society on its way to destruction. It is possible to prize marriage without censuring any of the alternative conditions in which mature adults find themselves.

It is possible to praise marriage as an institution while accepting, indeed condoning, the action taken by partners in failed marriages to break out and away.

Perhaps Tony Blair and John Major and their acolytes, despite their crude, self-interested and often ridiculous pronunciamentos, are on to something. It is not necessarily public anxiety about the general direction of change of mores or behaviour; rather, there may be a latent regret that too few leaders speak up for institutions that ordinary people know from within to be worthy of a stout defence. Opinion polls pick up surface movements. We know little about the dynamic of those deeper movements in sensibility which, certainly in the post-war world, have by and large, moved Britain in a more civilised, more liberal and more tolerant direction. But now the feeling seems to be that there are certain irreplaceable elements in the married state. The cult of single equals free equals happy is fast losing its allure.

Culture seems to have fallen behind. Younger women write boldly of their quest for freedom and self-realisation which, they proudly say, has no place in it for traditional man-woman marriage, or even its solemnised variants. Novels, films, television series, newspaper stories, mostly glamorise and celebrate singlehood. How far back (to *Middlemarch*?) do we need to go to find a serious prolonged fictional account of the state of marriage in which the marital state (mutual fidelity, mutual struggle) is treated as at least as interesting and important and exciting as adultery and getting your leg over? The downside gets play from poets, (marriage from love, like vinegar from wine, said Byron), film-makers and scriptwriters. The upside of the single life, meanwhile, excites the songwriters, with their fixation on brief erotic passion.

And yet the attractions of the married condition nag away. A note of regret and longing to be settled with a loving partner rings through the feisty tale of our own iconic single woman, Bridget Jones. In the real world, marriage offers security, stability, the attractions of predictable intimacy. Marriage is where rules of good conduct are learnt, where participation in economic life gets its essential supports, where the generation to come is socialised.

Marriage deserves a better break, in fiscal as well as social policy terms. Not all choices in relationships are emotional. Some are based on calculations of cost. Living together, getting married and having children all cut disposable income. Were it not for her hopeless political partisanship, a think-tanker such as Patricia

Morgan of the Institute of Economic Affairs would deserve a much wider hearing on the inequity of the married state in the eyes of the government. Perhaps in an ideal world the state would be neutral, ensuring that men and women with children were left no worse off in terms of post-tax (and benefits) income. We are a long way from that.

In the meantime, much can be done to redress a cultural imbalance that has left marriage with too few convincing advocates. The moral authoritarians kill their own message with bug-eyed ranting. They insist, wrongly, that valuing domestic arrangements is a zero sum game in which admiring one necessarily means misprizing others, such as long term relationships between gays, or the natural solitary. To talk up marriage is not – this is a critical point – some backhand way of redefining the role of women. Even if women's sensibility had not permanently changed, and it has, women are now too central as players in the modern economy for that even to be a thinkable project.

Marriage has evolved over the years, and is capable of further change, in terms of the domestic division of labour, child care, housework, and the rest. But at its heart remains a constant union of two people for whom affection translates naturally into life in a joint household in which the other is, for better or for worse, predictably there. Not all single people yearn for that emotional stability; many married people are deeply frustrated within it. But most people aspire to it, and they do so with very good reason. We should find better ways to reinforce and applaud such unions, wherever, and whenever and however they succeed.

Leader, The *Independent*, 29 October 1996

In a leader last week the *Guardian* perversely praised the new statement of values for schools, because it didn't promote 'the traditional cornflake version of a heterosexual married couple and their children'. I despair.

This is, in fact, by far the most usual kind of family. It is also the best kind for the people who matter most – the children. Every piece of serious research confirms this.

Today, an authoritative report, funded by the Joseph Rowntree Association, confirms that 'the traditional family is still the norm'. The study, *Parenting in the 1990's*, checked out 6000 mothers and fathers, all in their early 30's. Threequarters of them were married.

This is not a gee-whizz discovery, like the proof, someday, of life on Mars. But it is astonishing how resistant many commentators are to the idea that the traditional family is alive and well. Left and right, in unholy matrimony, join together to assert the opposite. The left is driven by the assumption that the family somehow trammels individual self-expression. The right fears, as always, that society is about to collapse. They are both wrong.

The much debated rise in lone parenthood is, mostly, a mirage. And the usual conclusions drawn from the fashion for cohabitation are misleading. The bare statistics are snapshots. But life is more like a movie than a snapshot. Things don't stay frozen. Typically, life as a lone parent lasts for only about three and a half years. (According to a Policy Studies Institute survey last year).

Cohabitation is equally transient. It 'is usually a prelude to marriage,' and it is 'becoming an institutionalised part of the mating process, in the same way that the period of engagement used to be' (Family Policy Studies Centre report 1993).

This scarcely signals the decline and fall of the 'cornflake version' of the family. Which is fortunate for both Kellogg's and for our children.

The good news is that, despite the widespread impression to the contrary, four out of five children currently live in a two parent family (Social Trends, 1996). This is fortunate, because all studies show that, on average, children are better off in a traditional family, less likely to be ill, poorly fed, or in trouble at school. Of course there are exceptions. Money can ease the risks. Contrariwise, traditional families can fail. But the average remains stubbornly the same, it is a question of the odds. These are stacked against children who are not in traditional families. And 'traditional' not only means parents who are together, but stay together. An Exeter University study has interviewed children whose parents separated or divorced. It compared them with similar children whose parents had not. The children in the split-up families had 'a reduced sense of their own worth'. They had more sickness. They found it harder to make friends. Divorce, the study found, was worse for the children than continuing to live with parents who had rows, or even fought. Most children said, 'they wished their parents had stayed together.'

The evidence is overwhelming. A recent Scottish study interviewed 1000 young people. Those who were still living with both their natural parents at the age of 15 were at the least risk of being caught up in the drug culture or falling into unemployment. The girls were less likely to become teenage mothers, or to leave school without any qualifications.

Sometimes, in thinking about the condition of marriage in contemporary Britain, we simply fail to take a long enough historical look. A higher percentage of the population is married now than a century ago. Sometimes we get bogged down in trying not to be criticised for being 'racist' or some other variety of 'ist'.

For example, nine out of ten parents are white. That said, black children are disproportionately likely to be living with lone parents. The 1991 census showed that more than 40% of black children, (that is Caribbean or African,) live with a lone parent. This contrasts with less than 10% of Asian children, and about 15% of white children. I cannot see that it does anybody any good to veer away from confronting the disadvantages this brings.

Consider the relative success of children of Indian origin who have settled in Britain. The census shows that they are better off, better educated and better housed than the equivalent members of the white population.

Mightn't this have something to do with their extremely cohesive family life? Or must we sneer at the chapati family as well as the cornflake family?

Now undoubtedly all this has uncomfortable implications for some brands of liberal. But they can be summed up in a single phrase: always think of the children. At present, every year, more than fifty thousand children under the age of five have parents who divorce. The numbers have been rising. That is the real threat. Parents have put themselves first.

Marriage, down the centuries, has gone through various stages. To begin with, you could argue that it was mostly economic. A man acquired a woman who, if not a chattel slave, was, nevertheless a kind of property. She 'belonged' in every sense to her husband. She helped most families stay afloat, either through her dowry or through her labour, or both.

More recently we have decided that marriage should unceasingly give the man and the woman deep personal satisfaction. But trouble follows if this is the absolute touchstone. It seems, sometimes, that husbands and wives behave like children themselves. If they can't have everything, then they walk.

It may be time to move to a more ecological ideal of marriage: marriage as a nest. This doesn't mean that we have to go around moralising endlessly about people who live differently. But it does mean that we should be clear where the balance of advantage lies. For the children's sake.

Paul Barker, The *Guardian*, 4 November 1996

21. Writers and Writing

Critics and Criticism

A malignant deity, called Criticism ... At her right hand sat Ignorance, her father and husband, blind with age; at her left, Pride, her mother, dressing her up in scraps of paper she herself had torn. There was Opinion, her sister, light of foot, hoodwinked, and headstrong, yet giddy and perpetually turning. About her played her children, Noise and Impudence, Dullness and Vanity, Positiveness, Pedantry and Ill-Manners.

The Goddess herself had claws like a cat, her head, and ears, and voice resembled those of an ass; her teeth fallen out before, her eyes turned inward, as if she also looked only upon herself; her diet was the overflowing of her own gall.

Jonathan Swift (1667–1745)

A critic has remarked that had I selected another method of composition and taken a little more trouble the tale could have been told in about two hundred pages. I confess I do not perceive exactly the bearings of such criticism or even the use of such a remark. No doubt that by selecting a certain method and taking great pains the whole story might have been written out on a cigarette paper. For that matter, the whole history of mankind could be written thus if only approached with sufficient detachment. The history of men on this earth since the beginning of ages may be resumed in one phrase of infinite poignancy: They were born, they suffered, they died ... Yet it is a great tale! But in the infinitely minute stories about men and women it is my lot on earth to narrate I am not capable of such detachment.

What makes this book memorable to me apart from the natural sentiment one has for one's creation is the response it provoked. The general public responded largely, more largely perhaps than to any other book of mine, in the only way the general public can respond, that is by buying a certain number of copies. This gave me a considerable amount of pleasure, because what I always feared most was drifting unconsciously into the position of a writer for a limited coterie: a position which would have been odious to me as throwing a doubt on the soundness of my belief in the solidarity of all mankind in simple ideas and in sincere emotions. Regarded as a manifestation of criticism (for it would be outrageous to deny to the general public the possession of a critical mind) the reception was very satisfactory. I saw that I had managed to please a certain number of minds busy attending to their own very real affairs. It is agreeable to think one is able to please. From the minds whose business it is precisely to criticize such attempts to please, this book received an amount of discussion and of a rather searching analysis which not only satisfied that personal vanity I share with the rest of mankind but reached my deeper feelings and aroused my gratified interest. The undoubted sympathy informing the varied appreciations of that book was, I love to think, a recognition of my good faith in the pursuit of my art – the art of the novelist which a distinguished French writer at the end of a successful career complained of as being: *Trop difficile*. It is indeed *too* arduous in the sense that the effort must be invariably so much greater than the possible achievement. In that sort of foredoomed task which is in its nature very lonely also, sympathy is a precious thing. It can make the most severe criticism welcome. To be told that better things have been expected of one may be soothing in view of how much better things one had expected from oneself in this art which, in these days, is no longer justified by the assumption, somewhere and somehow, of a didactic purpose.

I do not mean to hint that anybody had ever done me the injury (I don't mean insult, I mean injury) of charging a single one of my pages with didactic purpose. But every subject in the region of intellect and emotion must have a morality of its own if it is treated at all sincerely; and even the most artful of writers will give himself (and his morality) away in about every third sentence. The varied shades of moral significance which have been discovered in my writings are very numerous. None of them, however, have provoked a hostile manifestation. It may have happened to me to sin against taste now and then, but apparently I have never sinned against the basic feelings and elementary convictions which make life possible to the mass of mankind and, by establishing a standard of judgement, set their idealism free to look for plainer ways, for higher feelings, for deeper purposes.

I cannot say that any particular moral complexion has been put on this novel but I do not think that anybody had detected in it an evil intention. And it is only for their intentions that men can be held responsible. The ultimate effects of whatever they do are far beyond their control. In doing this book my intention was to interest people in my vision of things which is indissolubly allied to the style in which it is expressed. In other words I wanted to write a certain amount of pages in prose, which, strictly speaking, is my proper business. I have attended to it conscientiously with the hope of being entertaining or at least not insufferably boring to my readers. I can not sufficiently insist upon the truth that when I sit down to write my intentions are always blameless however deplorable the ultimate effect of the act may turn out to be.

Joseph Conrad (1857–1924), from 'Author's Notes' on his novel,
Chance

Inspiration

Can anyone at the end of this nineteenth century possibly have any distinct notion of what poets of a more vigorous period meant by inspiration? If not, I should like to describe it. Provided one has the slightest remnant of superstition left, one can hardly reject completely the idea that one is the mere incarnation, or mouthpiece, or medium of some almighty power. The notion of revelation describes the condition quite simply; by which I mean that something profoundly convulsive and disturbing suddenly becomes visible and audible with indescribable definiteness and exactness. One hears – one does not seek; one takes – one does not ask who gives: a thought flashes out like lightning, inevitably without hesitation – I have never had any choice about it.

Friedrich Nietzsche (1844–1900), *Thus Spake Zarathustra*, 1883

A man finds out that there is somewhat in him that knows more than he does. Then he comes presently to the curious question, who's who? Which of these two is really me? The one who knows more or the one who knows less? The little fellow or the big fellow?

Ralph Waldo Emerson, Journal 1859, undated

Songwriting is about getting the demon out of me. It's like being possessed. You try to go to sleep, but the song won't let you. So you have to get up and make it into something, and then you're allowed to sleep. It's always in the middle of the bloody night, or when you're half awake or tired, when your critical faculties are switched off. So letting go is what the whole game is.

John Lennon (1940–80) from 'Influencing Minds',
Leonard Roy Frank, 1995

May I not be forgiven for thinking it is a wonderful testimony to my being made for art, that when in the midst of this trouble and pain I sit down to my book, some beneficent power shows it all to me and tempts me to be interested, and I don't invent it – really do not – but *see* it and write it down.

Charles Dickens (1812–70), letter to his biographer, John Forster

It is a strange process to me, writing. It starts with excitement and enthusiasm and goes through a variety of phases which range from comfortable and indulgent research, to bitter regret that I ever committed myself to this particular project. The 'research' phase, is perhaps the most enjoyable, when nothing much gets written apart from pages of notes, carefully filed and never referred to again. Then deadlines creep up on me, and desperation seeps into my soul, a terrible fear that I have actually forgotten how to write. Its grip is insidious, it wraps itself around my brain, a serpent that eventually sinks its fangs into my neck and sends panic surging through my veins, until I realise the awful truth that there is nothing left to do, but actually *start* writing. And then the miracle happens as I watch the words appear, and I am reminded once again that the physical business of putting words on to a page is, in itself, a creative process.

Usually I write and rewrite a great deal, with the exception of one book, a book called, *An Impossible God*, which seemed to write itself. Maybe it was the environment. We were living on a hill farm in North Wales at the time, on the Llyn peninsula, almost at the foot of the Yr Eifl mountains. A place where clouds swirled around mysterious peaks and formed fantastic patterns, cloaks for mythical giants who tossed them over their shoulders as they stepped across the valleys. I was ill at the time, in that I couldn't walk very far. I was visited by Sarah Baird Smith, who was a commissioning editor for Collins at that time. She, her husband Robin, and their children came up to Tyn Y Gors, our little farm, and she asked me to write a book. When I asked her, 'What about?' she said, 'Anything you like.' Which was really rather extraordinary when I think about it.

Perhaps some psychological fusion point had been reached when all the research, all the reading, talking, arguing, thinking and praying that I had ever done on the subject of the Passion had suddenly come together. I had never written anything so fast before. The words seemed to tumble on to the page.

I was sitting at a window set into a wall of a Welsh Longhouse, a ragged and rough edged stone wall, at least two feet deep. The window framed a view of farmyard, garden and fields.

Close to the window I could see cobwebs in a hedge, sometimes glistening and glittering with dew, in the distance, the sky and those dramatic Welsh clouds. The characters appeared before me in that window frame, and I wrote down what they said. I was writing in long-hand, and June, my wife, was typing each page as I wrote it, but she couldn't keep up, I seemed to be writing faster than she could type. If any book of mine ever 'wrote itself' this one did. Though, I don't know. I used to think that this was the only book I had ever written this way, but my wife says that the 'gestation' period of any book I write is always long and tortuous, but after I have finished what she calls, 'mulling', the actual writing usually happens fairly fast. So what do I know?

Frank Topping, BBC Broadcast, 1997

Poetry

Read the poems you like reading. Don't bother whether they're important, or if they'll live. What does it matter what poetry *is*, after all? If you want a definition of poetry, say: 'Poetry is what makes me laugh or cry or yawn, what makes my toenails twinkle, what makes me want to do this or that or nothing,' and let it go at that. All that matters about poetry is the enjoyment of it, however tragic it may be. All that matters is the eternal movement behind it, the vast under-current of human grief, folly, pretension, exaltation, or ignorance, however unlofty the intention of the poem.

You can tear a poem apart to see what makes it technically tick, and say to yourself, when the works are laid out before you, the vowels, the consonants, the rhymes and rhythms, 'Yes, this is *it*. This is why the poem moves me so. It is because of the craftsmanship.' But you're back again where you began. You're back with the mystery of having been moved by words. The best craftsmanship always leaves holes and gaps in the works of the poem so that something that is *not* in the poem can creep, crawl, dash, or thunder in.

The Way We Are

The joy and function of poetry is, and was, the celebration of
man, which is also the celebration of God.

Dylan Thomas, 'Notes on the Art of Poetry'

Part 3 Religion

22. Asceticism

The black shadow of asceticism spread over the sky of the Puritan Fathers. Given two coats, they chose the ugliest one. Given two colours for the women's garb, they chose the saddest and most sombre. Given two roads, they chose the one that held the most thorns and cutting rocks. Given two forms of fear and self-denial, they took both. The favourite text of asceticism is 'deny yourself.' The favourite colour of asceticism is black; its favourite music, a dirge; its favourite hour is midnight; its favourite theme is a tombstone. The mistake of asceticism is in thinking that it has a moral value.

Newell Dwight Hillis (1858–1939)

If there is no element of asceticism in our lives, if we give free rein to the desires of the flesh . . . we shall find it hard to train for the service of Christ.

Dietrich Bonhoeffer (1906–45)

23. Bishops

The crisis of the Church of England is that too many of its bishops, and some would say its archbishops, don't quite realise that they are atheists, but have begun to suspect it.

Clive James, *The Dreaming Swimmer* 1992

On the proposal for a Methodist episcopacy, in 1969, including a reference to a meeting in Lichfield in 1794 at which leading figures in the Methodist Connexion devised a plan for the appointment of Methodist Bishops and proposed themselves as candidates for office.

I believe we should seize this opportunity to restore the centre of gravity to our Church, where it should always have been but where perhaps it no longer is, at the point of pastoral care, of shepherding the flock. It would, it seems to me, to be fatal to begin with any ex-officio bishops, certainly not ex-presidents, or connexional officials, or college tutors. I don't believe our corridors of power and ambition are very large or very sinister, but at least let us rid ourselves of even the faintest reproach that these had any entrance in our midst. [Remember Lichfield!]

We might perhaps have room after a bit for a scholar or an administrator or two, but not at the beginning. Nor would I for the most part choose Chairmen of Districts – though as far as in them lies they are fulfilling a true pastoral bishop's office. But . . . I should look for bishops at the place where historically our pastoral care has centred, to Superintendent ministers, the kind who get on with their colleagues, really look after their young ministers, and are respected and loved by their people . . . I imagine the situation would be like that in the early Celtic Church, when the administration was monastic, in the hands of abbots, and bishops were just kept to ordain – for breeding purposes, so to speak.

The Rev. Dr Gordon Rupp, former president of the Methodist Conference and principal of Wesley College, Cambridge

24. Celestial Bodies

Now as to celestial phenomena, we must believe that these motions, periods, eclipses, risings, settings, and the like do not take place because there is some divinity in charge of them, who so arranges them in order and will maintain them in that order, and who at the same time enjoys both perfect happiness and immortality; for activity and anxiety, anger and kindness are not in harmony with blessedness, but are found along with weakness, fear and dependence on one's neighbours. We must also avoid the belief that masses of concentrated fire have attained a state of divine blessedness and undertaken these motions of their own free will . . .

In addition to these general matters, we must observe this also, that there are three things that account for the major disturbances in men's minds. First, they assume that celestial bodies are blessed and eternal yet have impulses, actions, and purposes quite inconsistent with divinity. Next, they anticipate and foresee eternal punishment as depicted in the myths, or even fear the very lack of consciousness that comes with death as if this could be of concern to them. Finally, they suffer all this, not as a result of reasonable conjecture, but through some sort of unreasoning imagination; and since in imagination they set no limit to suffering, they are beset by turmoil as great as if there were a reasonable basis for their dread, or even greater. But it is peace of mind to have been freed from all this and to have constantly in memory the essential principles of the whole system of belief. We must therefore turn our minds to immediate feelings and sensations – in matters of general concern to the common feelings and sensation of mankind, in personal matters, to our own – and to every immediate evidence from each of the means of judgement. If we heed these, we shall rightly track down the sources of disturbance and fear, and when we have learned the causes of celestial phenomena and of the other occasional happenings, we shall be free from what other men most dread.

Epicurus, *c*. 300 BC

25. Chance or Providence

As some divinely gifted man,
Whose life in low estate began
And on a simple village green;

Who breaks his birth's invidious bar,
And grasps the skirts of happy chance,
and breasts the blows of circumstance
And grapples with his evil star.

Alfred, Lord Tennyson (1809–92), from 'In the Valley of Cauteretz'

'. . . I didn't even know that much of him. All I knew of him was an accident called Fyne.'

At this Mr. Powell, who evidently could be rebellious, too, turned his back squarely on the window.

'What on earth do you mean?' he asked, 'An accident – called Fyne,' he repeated, separating the words with emphasis.

Marlowe was not disconcerted.

'I don't mean accident in the sense of a mishap. Not in the least. Fyne was a good little man in the civil service. By accident I mean that which happens blindly and without intelligent design. That's generally the way a brother-in-law happens into a man's life.'

Joseph Conrad (1857–1924), *Chance*

'Listen Powell,' I said. 'We got to know each other by chance?'
   'Oh quite!' he admitted, adjusting his hat.
   'And the science of life consists in seizing every chance that
presents itself,' I pursued. 'Do you believe that?'
   'Gospel truth,' he declared innocently.
   'Well, don't forget it.'

                                  Joseph Conrad (1857–1924), *Chance*

*Simon of Cyrene, speaking of meeting Jesus by 'chance' on the Via
Dolorosa:*

          Chosen,
          or merely ill-fated?
          And what's the difference?
          Is there a line
          between the vagaries of
          chance and providence?
          A division between accident
          and an act of God?
          And does the difference lie
          not in the event
          but in the man?

          A terrified man in a garden
          has nothing but fear in his nostrils,
          though the scent of the rose
          has not diminished,
          nor its bloom.

          God help me,
          God was there
          on the streets of Jerusalem.
          but I did not perceive him
          in that miasma of malice.
          There is nothing spiritual
          in the stench of a mob.
          I tell you,

and the air was foul
with the reek of lust,
lust for blood.
And I did not see God in the event.
I saw only the threat
and the danger to myself.

Who expects his whole life to change
by accident?
Well, no one expects, but it happens,
accidents of time and place.

It's a long way from Cyrene
to the Damascus Gate.
Do you know how long?
Well, it's not much short
of a thousand miles.
And there's no easy way.

Camels in the wilderness,
mules in the mountains,
not much protection
from thieves and brigands,
even if you pay.
And we couldn't pay
so we obeyed the rules
of the caravan traveller.

   – Don't trail behind,
   – stay with the crowd,
   – and sleep back to back,
   – with your eyes open!

By sea to Joppa
might have been quicker,
if we'd worked our passage,
survived storm, pirates
and rotten timbers.

Religion

But I like to feel the earth
beneath my feet.
So I trekked a thousand miles
to arrive at that street corner,
on that day,
at that precise minute.
Now there's accident,
there's chance for you.

With cruel precision,
random elements of circumstance
converge at that moment.
Jesus stumbles.
Mary, aged by his pain
mutely implores the soldier.
The soldier, for a confusion of reasons
decides,
and at that moment,
me, Simon,
the convenient foreigner
arrives.
Random elements, did I say?
Strange isn't it,
how the unpredicted and unrelated
blend,
effortlessly.

Not Roman enough to matter,
not Jewish enough to offend,
not local enough to shame,
a rough kindness in the soldier's choice.
But for me, the fear,
shouldering that beam.
Even the *memory* of it
shrinks my stomach.

Here I Stand

I cursed my luck,
I sweated, I watched.
I wept, and yet,
and yet,
I would not trade
one drop
of that day's sweat.

Frank Topping, 'Simon of Cyrene' from *An Impossible God*

26. Convictions

'Here I stand, I can do no other.' Martin Luther at the Diet of Worms, 1521

The excommunication of Martin Luther in the Papal Bull 'Exsurge Domine' was published in Saxony in the autumn of 1520. The Elector refused to carry it out and Luther repudiated the Pope and burnt the Bull publicly. In January 1521 the Pope issued another, stronger Bull and called on the Emperor to put it into effect. A Diet was summoned and Luther was given his chance to recant. He was asked by Eck, an official of the Archbishop of Trier, 'Do you wish to defend the books which are recognised as your work? Or to retract anything contained in them?' Luther replied:

Most Serene Lord Emperor, Most Illustrious Princes, Most Gracious Lords . . . I beseech you to grant a gracious hearing to my plea, which, I trust, will be a plea of justice and truth; and if through my inexperience I neglect to give to any their proper titles or in any way offend against the etiquette of the court in my manners or behaviour, be kind enough to forgive me, I beg, since I am a man who has spent his life not in courts but in the cells of a monastery; a man who can say of himself only this, that to this day; I have thought and written in simplicity of heart, solely with a view to the glory of God and the pure instruction of Christ's faithful people . . .

Your Imperial Majesty and Your Lordships: I ask you to observe that my books are not all of the same kind.

There are some in which I have dealt with piety in faith and morals with such simplicity and so agreeably with the Gospels that my adversaries themselves are compelled to admit them useful, harmless, and clearly worth reading by a Christian. Even the Bull, harsh and cruel though it is, makes some of my books harmless, although it condemns them also, by a judgement downright monstrous. If I should begin to recant here, what, I beseech you, should I be doing but condemning, alone among mortals, that truth which is admitted by friends and foes alike, in an unaided struggle against universal consent?

The second kind consists in those writings levelled against the papacy and the doctrine of the papists, as against those who by their wicked doctrines and precedents have laid waste Christendom by doing harm to the souls and the bodies of men. No one can either deny or conceal this, for universal experience and worldwide grievances are witnesses to the fact that through the Pope's laws and through man-made teachings the consciences of the faithful have been most pitifully ensnared, troubled, and racked in torment, and also that their goods and possessions have been devoured (especially amongst this famous German nation) by unbelievable tyranny, and are to this day being devoured without end in shameful fashion; and that though they themselves by their own laws take care to provide that the Pope's laws and doctrines which are contrary to the Gospel or the teachings of the Fathers are to be considered as erroneous and reprobate. If then I recant these, the only effect will be to add strength to such tyranny, to open not the windows but the main doors to such blasphemy, which will thereupon stalk farther and more widely than it has hitherto dared.

The third kind consists of those books which I have written against private individuals, so-called; against those, that is, who have exerted themselves in defence of the Roman tyranny and to the overthrow of that piety which I have taught. I confess that I have been more harsh against them than befits my religious vows and my profession. For I do not make myself out to be any kind of saint, nor am I now contending about my conduct but about Christian doctrine. But it is not in my power to recant them, because that recantation would give that tyranny and blasphemy an occasion to lord it over those whom I defend and to rage against God's people more violently than ever.

However, since I am a man and not God, I cannot provide my writings with any other defence than that which my Lord Jesus Christ provided for his teaching when he had been interrogated concerning his teaching before Annas and had received a buffet from a servant, he said: 'If I have spoken evil, bear witness of the evil.' If the Lord himself who knew that he could not err, did not refuse to listen to witness against his teaching, even from a worthless slave, how much more ought I, scum that I am, capable of naught but error, to seek and to want for any who may wish to bear witness against my teaching.

And so, through the mercy of God, I ask Your Imperial Majesty, and Your Illustrious Lordships, or anyone of any degree, to bear witness, to overthrow my errors, to defeat them by the writings of the Prophets or by the Gospels; for I shall be most ready, if I be better instructed, to recant any error, and I shall be the first in casting my writings into the fire . . .

[Thereupon the 'Orator of the Empire', with ill-temper, said that his answer was not to the point, and that there should be no calling into question matters on which condemnations and decisions had earlier been passed by Councils. He was being asked for a plain reply, without subtlety or sophistry, to this question: Was he prepared to recant, or no? Luther then replied:]

Your Imperial Majesty and Your Lordships demand a simple answer. Here it is, plain and unvarnished. Unless I am convicted of error by the testimony of Scripture or (since I put no trust in the unsupported authority of Pope or of councils, since it is plain that they have often erred and often contradicted themselves) by manifest reasoning, I stand convicted by the Scriptures to which I have appealed, and my conscience is taken captive by God's word, I cannot and will not recant anything, for to act against our conscience is neither safe for us, nor open to us.

Here I stand. I can do no other. God help me. Amen.

Martin Luther (1483–1546)

A great deal of the letter to the Romans is a wonderfully argued statement of Paul's understanding of his faith, but this particular passage rings with both the depth of his spirituality and of his conviction.

The Spirit also understands our inadequacies. We do not know how to pray as we should, but the Spirit mediates for us with unutterable sighs. And he who searches our hearts knows the mind of the Spirit because the Spirit's prayers, on our behalf, are in tune with God's will.

We know that God works all things together for good, for those who love him, for those called according to his purpose. Those already called are also chosen to conform to the image of his son, so that he should be the firstborn of many. Those who are chosen he calls, and those he calls he vindicates, and those he vindicates, he also glorifies.

What shall we say to all this? If God is for us, who is against us? He did not deny us his own son but offered him for us all, giving us his son, how will he not give us all things?

Who will bring charges against those called by God? It is God who justifies, who will condemn? Christ Jesus is the one who having died, and having been raised, is at the right hand of God, pleading with him on our behalf.

So who will separate us from the love of Christ? Will affliction, or distress, or persecution, or famine, or nakedness, or peril, or sword? As it has been written, 'All day, we are being killed, for your sake, like sheep being slaughtered.'

But in all these things we are victorious through him who loved us. For I am convinced that neither death, nor life, nor angels, nor rulers, nor things present, nor things to come, nor powers, nor height, nor depth, nor any other creature will be able to separate us from the love of God in Christ Jesus, our Lord.

St Paul's Letter to the Romans, chapter 8, verses 26–39

27. Creeds

The Apostles' Creed

I believe in God, the Father almighty,
creator of heaven and earth.

I believe in Jesus Christ, his only Son, our Lord.
He was conceived by the power of the Holy Spirit
and born of the Virgin Mary.
He suffered under Pontius Pilate,
was crucified, died, and was buried.
He descended to the dead.
On the third day he rose again.
He ascended into heaven,
and is seated at the right hand of the Father.
He will come again to judge the living and the dead.

I believe in the Holy Spirit,
the holy catholic Church,
the communion of saints,
the forgiveness of sins,
the resurrection of the body,
and the life everlasting.

The Nicene Creed

We believe in one God,
the Father, the Almighty,
maker of heaven and earth,
of all that is, seen and unseen.

We believe in one Lord, Jesus Christ,
the only son of God,
eternally begotten of the Father,
God from God, Light from Light,
true God from true God,
begotten, not made,
of one Being with the Father.
Through him all things were made.
For us and for our salvation
he came down from heaven:
by the power of the Holy Spirit
he became incarnate from the Virgin Mary,
and was made man.

For our sake he was crucified under Pontius Pilate;
he suffered death and was buried.
On the third day he rose again
in accordance with the scriptures;
he ascended into heaven
and is seated at the right hand of the Father.
He will come again in glory
to judge the living and the dead,
and his kingdom will have no end.

We believe in the Holy Spirit, the Lord, the giver of life,
who proceeds from the Father and the Son.
With the Father and the Son he is worshipped and glorified.
He has spoken through the prophets.
We believe in one holy catholic and apostolic Church.
We acknowledge one baptism for the forgiveness of sins.
We look for the resurrection of the dead,
and the life of the world to come.

The Athanasian Creed

Whoever will be saved: before all things it is necessary that he hold the Catholick Faith.

Which faith except every one do keep whole and undefiled: without doubt he shall perish everlastingly.

And the Catholick Faith is this: That we worship one God in Trinity, and Trinity in Unity;

Neither confounding the Persons: nor dividing the Substance.

For there is one Person of the Father, another of the Son: and another of the Holy Ghost. But the Godhead of the Father, of the Son, and of the Holy Ghost, is all one: the Glory equal, the Majesty co-eternal.

Such as the Father is, such is the Son: and such is the Holy Ghost.

The Father uncreate, the Son uncreate: the Holy Ghost uncreate.

The Father incomprehensible, the Son incomprehensible: and the Holy Ghost incomprehensible.

The Father eternal, the Son eternal: and the Holy Ghost eternal.

And yet they are not three eternals: but one eternal.

As also there are not three incomprehensibles, nor three uncreated: but one uncreated, and one incomprehensible.

So likewise the Father is Almighty, the Son Almighty: and the Holy Ghost Almighty.

And yet there are not three Almighties: but one Almighty.

So the Father is God, the Son is God: and the Holy Ghost is God.

And yet there are not three Gods: but one God.

So likewise the Father is Lord, the Son is Lord: and the Holy Ghost Lord.

And yet not three Lords, but one Lord.

For like as we are compelled by the Christian verity: to acknowledge every Person by himself to be God and Lord;

So we are forbidden by the Catholick religion: to say, There be three Gods, or three Lords.

The Father is made of none: neither created, nor begotten.

The Son is of the Father alone: not made, nor created, but begotten.

The Holy Ghost is of the Father and of the Son: neither made, nor created, nor begotten, but proceeding.

So there is one Father, not three Fathers; one Son, not three Sons:

one Holy Ghost, not three Holy Ghosts.

And in this Trinity none is afore, or after other: none is greater, or less than another.

But the whole three Persons are co-eternal together: and co-equal.

So that in all things, as is aforesaid: The Unity in the Trinity, and the Trinity in the Unity is to be worshipped.

He therefore that will be saved: must thus think of the Trinity.

Furthermore, it is necessary to everlasting salvation: that he also believe rightly the Incarnation of our Lord Jesus Christ.

For right Faith is, that we believe and confess: that our Lord Jesus Christ, the Son of God, is God and Man;

God, of the substance of the Father, begotten before the worlds: the Man, of the substance of his Mother, born in the world;

Perfect God, and perfect Man: of a reasonable soul and human flesh subsisting;

Equal to the Father, as touching his Manhood.

Who although he be God and Man: yet he is not two, but one Christ;

One; not by the conversion of the Godhead into flesh: but by taking of the Manhood into God;

One altogether; not by confusion of Substance: but by unity of Person.

For as the reasonable soul and flesh is one man: So God and Man is one Christ;

who suffered for our salvation: descended into Hell, rose again the third day from the dead.

He ascended into heaven, he sitteth on the right hand of the Father, God Almighty:

from whence he shall come to judge the quick and the dead . . .

At whose coming all men shall rise again with their bodies: and shall give account for their own works.

And they that have done good shall go into life everlasting: and they that have done evil into everlasting fire.

This is the Catholick Faith which except a man believe faithfully, he cannot be saved.

Glory to the Father, and to the Son: and to the Holy Ghost;

As it was in the beginning, is now, and ever shall be: world without end. Amen.

28. Crucifixion

There is no fitting word
to describe a crucifixion,
or if there is,
it was conceived in Hell,
where, I trust,
God rots the soul
of the fiend who devised it.
Were I to paint a picture
of a crucifixion,
with executioners,
and ghoulish spectators,
it would be filled with devils,
diabolical spirits,
malevolent sprites,
cloven-hooved demons
who must surely dance
in an ecstasy of evil,
with Beelzebub presiding,
or Lucifer, or Satan,
or whatever name you choose
for the Prince of Darkness.
I'd rather fight a horde
of hairy Barbarians
than witness one crucifixion
in the so called 'line of duty'.
By the Gods!
It's a disgusting way to kill a man.

Here I Stand

Twelve years' Imperial Service
and the proud possessor
of a centurion's staff
and the oak-leaf crown
for gallantry in battle.
You don't need much gallantry
to supervise a gibbet
but by God you need oak-leaf courage
to die on one with dignity.
I've seen them weep,
struggle, scream and cry for mercy;
and stoics, in teeth-clenched silence
right to the end. I've saluted them.

Well, I have to be there, so I am there!

But the Galilean,
he was another question altogether.

The death of a criminal I understand,
and I lose no sleep over traitors,
but political guile,
assassination by dupery,
murder by manipulation,
that wrinkles the nostrils.
I could smell the stink
of their pious fraudulence.
Even though they stood
on the outer fringe,
I could see the grim satisfaction,
the covert looks and nods.
Through all the religious garb,
the priestly manners,
I could see their devious minds.
Treachery wafted from them
like the breeze from a stagnant pool.

Religion

I offered him the customary drink,
something to stupefy the pain,
though I know of no potion
to blur the viciousness of crucifixion.
They usually drain the cup.
The Galilean took it,
let it touch his lips
and then returned it.
Like a guest going through the motions
of courtesy.
He did it with such grace,
and looked at me so steadily,
I hesitated to proceed.
I could see the executioners
with their eyes on his robe,
like hungry dogs waiting for food.
He closed his eyes, quite briefly,
as if giving consent for me to continue.
I echoed that consent
and in seconds he stood naked
while the men, like scavengers,
searched for a seam to divide the cloth.
There was no seam,
so they diced for it.
And while they gambled
like gross, distorted urchins,
we looked,
not on his nakedness
but into his face.

Never a death like this,
and I've lost count.
Nor will I see its like again.
Dying men cling to life, you know,
even hanging on a cross.
Strong men can last for days.
For what? you might well ask.
Give up, get it over with,

that would make more sense.
But no, they usually struggle.
To see just one more dawn?
Hear a bird?
Feel the breeze,
hear a voice, just once more?
Or perhaps they hope beyond hope
for reprieve, to be taken down.
I don't know.
But they don't go easily.
They don't choose to go.
But he did.
His struggle wasn't with death.
Death was his servant,
not his master.
That wasn't a defeated man.
He was in command to the end.
And then, he gave up his spirit.
It wasn't taken from him,
he gave it up.
He fought a battle from the cross,
but not with death.

I never got to the bottom
of whatever trumped-up charges
put him on that gibbet,
but there wasn't a ghost of guilt about him.
Some said he was a prophet,
but he was more than that,
much more.
On the cross,
his conflict was with something far greater
than bitter-tongued Pharisees;
he ignored them,
as dross scattered in the wind.
No, he fought a different battle
and I caught something of it.
I could sense it.

Religion

I could almost smell it.

And when he cried out,
something in Hebrew I think,
as if he had been wounded,
I gripped my sword.
I would have fought
if I could have seen the enemy.
But he pulled through.
Later, he gave a great cry of victory.
They were puzzled,
but I know battles and fighters.
I'd recognize a victor's shout,
anywhere.

You do not expect nobility
in the squalor of a crucifixion,
it is meant to humiliate.
You do not expect magnanimity
in the face of cruelty,
pain usually erases that.
Solemnity splattered by obscenity.
Silence in a welter of abuse.
Dignity surviving malicious wounds.
You do not expect majesty to bleed from a cross,
nor a king to be enthroned on a scaffold,
but that is what these eyes witnessed,
the transformation of a bestial ceremony into a coronation.
If innocence could be seen
it was in his eyes.
If truth could be heard
it was in his voice.
If regality exists
it has his face.
If God exists
then this was his son.

Like courtiers,

they lifted down his body,
the cloak of sovereignty
entrusted to their care;
the ornate robe of the conqueror,
his sceptre and orb
temporarily laid aside.

Frank Topping, 'The Centurion' from *An Impossible God*

29. Faith in Adversity

If you carry the cross willingly, it will carry you.
If you are forced against your will to carry the cross,
then you make it difficult for yourself, adding to your load.
No matter what attitude you have, you must bear the burden.
If you manage to throw away one cross, you will certainly find
    another,
and it may be even heavier.

                                    Thomas à Kempis (*c.* 1380–1471)

When compassed about on every side with tribulations remember
that it is the way of the saints, through which they passed to the
kingdom of heaven. Learn to comfort thyself also, because that in
this thou art made like unto Christ Jesus, thy Lord; and return
thanks, if thou art in any small degree able to repay this to him.
For I say unto thee that it is a greater merit in thee to suffer
affliction patiently than to perform good works.

                                    Thomas à Kempis (*c.* 1380–1471)

We bring God to the bar of our judgement and say hard things
about him: 'Why does God bring thunderclouds and disasters
when we want green pastures and still waters?' Bit by bit we find,
behind the clouds, the Father's feet; behind the lightning, an
abiding day that has no night; behind the thunder a still, small
voice that comforts with a comfort that is unspeakable.

                                    Oswald Chambers (1874–1917)

The final declaration of the faith of Thomas Cranmer, Archbishop of Canterbury

Thomas Cranmer had spent almost three years in the Tower of London. On 21 March 1556, he signed the last of seven recantations in the hope that his life might be spared. His recantations made no difference. He was informed that he was to be burned at the stake that day. At the stake, he knelt and said the Lord's Prayer, then, with great courage he made this speech, retracting all his recantations and renouncing the Pope.

All men desire, good people, at the time of their deaths, to give some good exhortation that others may remember after their deaths, and be the better thereby. So I beseech God grant me grace that I may speak something, at this my departing, whereby God may be glorified and you edified.

First, it is an heavy ease to see that many folks be so much doted upon the love of this false world, and so careful for it, that for the love of God, or the love of the world to come, they seem to care very little or nothing therefore This shall be my first exhortation. That you set not overmuch by this false glozing world, but upon God and the world to come; and learn to know what this lesson meaneth, which St John teacheth, that the love of this world is hatred against God.

The second exhortation is that next unto God you obey your King and Queen willingly and gladly, without murmur and grudging and not for fear of them only, but much more for the fear of God knowing that they be God's ministers, appointed by God to rule and govern you. And therefore whoso resisteth them, resisteth God's ordinance.

The third exhortation is, That you love altogether like brethren and sisters. For, alas! pity it is to see what contention and hatred one Christian man hath toward another; not taking each other as sisters and brothers, but rather as strangers and mortal enemies. But I pray you learn and bear well away this one lesson, To do good to all men as much as in you lieth, and to hurt no man, no more than you would hurt your own natural and loving brother or sister. For this you may be sure of, that whosoever hateth any person, and goeth about maliciously to hinder or hurt him, surely, and without all doubt, God is not with that man, although he think himself never so much in God's favour.

The fourth exhortation shall be to them that have great substance and riches of this world, that they will well consider and weigh those sayings of the Scripture. One is of our Saviour Christ himself, who sayeth, it is hard for a rich man to enter into heaven; a sore saying, and yet spoken by him that knew the truth. The second is of St John, whose saying is this, He that hath the substance of this world and seeth his brother in necessity, and shutteth up his mercy from him, how can he say he loveth God? Much more might I speak of every part; but time sufficeth not. I do but put you in remembrance of these things. Let all them that be rich ponder well those sentences; for if ever they had any occasion to show their charity they have now at this present, the poor people being so many, and victuals so dear. For though I have been long in prison, yet I have heard of the great penury of the poor. Consider that which is given to the poor is given to God whom we have not otherwise present corporally with us, but in the poor.

And now, for so much as I am come to the last end of my life, whereupon hangeth all my life passed and my life to come, either to live with my Saviour Christ in heaven in joy, or else to be in pain ever with wicked devils in hell; and I see before mine eyes presently either heaven ready to receive me, or hell ready to swallow me up; I shall therefore declare unto you my very faith, how I believe, without colour or dissimulation; for now is no time to dissemble, whatsoever I have written in times past.

First, I believe in God the Father Almighty, Maker of heaven and earth, and every article of the catholic faith, every word and sentence taught by our Saviour Christ, His Apostles and Prophets, in the Old and New Testaments.

And now I come to the great thing that troubleth my conscience, more than any other thing that ever I said or did in my life; and that is, the setting abroad of writings contrary to the truth. Which here now I renounce and refuse, as things written with my hand, contrary to the truth which I thought in my heart, and writ for fear of death, and to save my life, if it might be; and that is, all such bills, which I have written or signed with mine own hand since my degradation, wherein I have written many things untrue. And forasmuch as my hand offended in writing contrary to my heart, therefore my hand shall be punished; for if I may come to the fire it shall be first burned. And as for the Pope, I refuse him as Christ's enemy and Anti-christ with all his false doctrine.

Thomas Cranmer, 21 March 1556

30. God

━━━━━━━━━━━━━━━━━━━━━━━━━━━━━━━━━━━━━━

Belief

After 10 years of writing about religion for a living, I realise that almost everything worthwhile I know about the subject I learnt in the first three months, when I realised that intelligent, educated and honest people could actually believe all that stuff. This was not an insight I was ever very successful in sharing with my colleagues. It may well have biased my reporting of the subject: intelligent, educated and scrupulously honest people are not a majority among the religious any more than they are among the pagans. But if you're going to spend 10 years of your life writing about one set of beliefs, it helps to make it tolerable if you suppose that these beliefs are worthwhile and might even be true.

It's not that I ever much doubted the existence of God. Everyone younger than 50 (except, apparently, Tony Blair) knows that he is only ever an inhalation away. A sense of something which is simultaneously the ultimate mystery and the ultimate meaning is a common part of human experience even among *Independent* readers. It is possible to go further than that. At a Bosnian monastery, the scene of unspeakable atrocities in the Second World War, I got zapped by the Holy Spirit and wandered around in a state of slippery joy for hours, forgiving not only my enemies but even the friendly Brummy Irish pilgrims who had been trying to convert me for a week. And I often think that if there were no Christians left in the world, I would have to become one. But then something happens. Often enough it is that I open the Bible. Every time someone praises 'Biblical morality' I want to ask them whether they have actually read the book. Perhaps on the 500th reading the civilised bits come through. But unless you have actually been brought up with it, so that its absurdities, like those of relatives, become part of the furniture of your mind, it is not a work to inspire confidence.

Then there are Christians. So many of them seem to go out of their way to demonstrate the sheer impossibility of believing what they do. This morning my local East Anglia paper included the following reflections from the Rev David Jebson: 'Gardeners appear cruel, especially when they're pruning and so God is sometimes misunderstood, especially when He allows suffering. Happily, those who acquiesce in His wisdom display the choice fruits of the Spirit, love, joy, patience, peace, etc.

'Make sure Jesus is the gardener of your soul, then one day he will transplant you to heaven!'

Another obstacle to belief is meeting saints. I had been really looking forward to meeting Mother Teresa, and when we were finally introduced, she took my hand, looked me straight in the eye and said: 'Tell your readers that contraception murders love.' Well, I thought: she's wrong about that; why should she be right about anything else? Of course she might have found something less ridiculous to say had she not known that I was a journalist. It may be thought a privilege to dash around meeting spiritual leaders but, as a journalist, you almost invariably meet people at their most banal and unimpressive. This is especially true when there are only the two of you present, because that almost always takes place in the context of an interview, which is usually a transaction with a stranger that belongs in short-stay hotel rooms.

Much better, if you want to sympathise with people, is to watch them at work; and this is something a news journalist hardly ever does. Of course with religion the difficulties are multiplied by asking what exactly the work of the religious is. If the answer to that question is 'prayer', it is an activity I cannot observe from the outside any more than I could report a chess world championship from the point of the players. I might record the moves accurately, but I could have little idea of why they were played. Fortunately, a lot of the work of religions does not involve prayer. I have seen the Dalai Lama expounding the finer points of Tibetan theology – and revealing far more of himself than ever when he was talking

English on subjects that I understood. I have watched the Pope working crowds, which is impressive; and have watched him working probably the smallest and least sympathetic audiences of his entire pontificate, which was much more impressive. That was in Finland, where the woman from one of the Helsinki papers leaned over to me at a cathedral service, and said, 'I have put on stockings and a garter belt for the first time in protest against his attitude to women. Feel!'

She had, too. The point of this story is not that Catholicism and sex are closely intertwined, but that it is often necessary to go abroad to discover just how strangely mixed are the bundles of beliefs and attitudes that we call religions. This is actually a very serious difficulty. The more time I spend writing about religions, the less certain I become what they are. There is a superstition around that any belief in metaphysical entities is religious. But I have met many atheists and no one who does not believe in abstract ideas. But as soon as you try to decide which beliefs are necessary for religion, you run into difficulties. Not even a belief in God is required. Buddhism, for example, can be a completely atheistic religion, but it can also involve an entire heavenly bureaucracy. Monotheism everywhere grows saints like a rock grows barnacles; quite often the underlying rock disappears at once. Some religions, like Judaism, revolve around practices, rather than particular beliefs; to be a Catholic it seems you don't even have to do anything, so long as you feel guilty afterwards.

Of course, that joke is just another example of the way in which the salient fact about Catholicism, at least for journalistic purposes, is that it has weird sexual mores. I don't actually know any Catholics for whom sex is the most important part of their religion (except for professional purposes) yet that kind of distortion seems built in to the way that journalists approach strange beliefs. We are always taking two-dimensional views of three-dimensional belief systems. I don't think this is a vice confined to journalists; it's just that we get paid for indulging it, whereas the rest of the world misunderstands for pleasure.

This matters especially with things like fundamentalism. The more fundamentalists I have known, the more I have liked them as people, and the more deeply I have reprehended their beliefs. I remember a missionary who drove me around Romania. He had been working in that part of the world since long before the collapse of Communism, smuggling Bibles, shipping food, clothing and generally relieving more suffering in a week than I manage in a year. 'I'm a fundamentalist, of course,' he said in the tone of someone mentioning that he had two legs. He probably did believe that the Earth was only 6,000 years old. The point was that this seemed to him a completely unimportant question. It was right out on the periphery of his world-view, so far as I could tell. It followed from his moral convictions rather than determining them, and the well-springs of his actions had nothing to do with astrophysical theories. To concentrate on them was to take quite the wrong slice through his complicated bundle of beliefs.

The complexity of religions explains, I believe, why I have never been able seriously to entertain the claim that non-Christian religions might be true. From time to time Buddhism, or the Judaism expounded by a liberal rabbi of my acquaintance, seem to be much the most sensible and civilised ways of approaching the universe. But without marrying into them, or otherwise weaving them into my personal, three-dimensional life, I could not possibly enter into them. Christianity is the myth I was brought up in and in which I was entirely at home until puberty, when a travelling evangelist converted me to the electric guitar.

I know there is not and could not be any axiomatic way to choose between Christianity and Buddhism, or Islam and Scientology: all are equally distant from scientifically establishable fact. But then so is any large statement about the purpose of the universe. It is demonstrably absurd to claim that the universe is meaningless. Either meaning is a category that human beings impose on an alien environment, in which case to say that the universe independent of human beings lacks meaning makes as little sense as saying that it is ultimately unfashionable or green or Swedish. But if, on the other hand, meaning is an independent quality that was there before us and will survive us, then QED.

And the search for meaning, or pattern, or beauty – the three seem intimately connected – is obviously a fundamental human drive, well below the surface of consciousness. It is so widespread that I cannot believe it hasn't got some kind of survival value; it seems to be part of the genetically determined tool kit of human thought, like an ability to count. 'Thou hast created us for Thyself and our heart is not quiet until it rests in Thee.' And it is possible to know exactly what he means while at the same time seeing its untruth.

The religious imagination is not a fixed quantity: it can be developed or stunted; in some people it seems to be the only form of imagination; in others it is hardly there at all. But this is true of all human faculties, from eyesight to mathematics. It does not make us doubt the truth of what we see, or of arithmetic. And even if the truth of Christianity does evanesce when looked at straight, it is still plainly to be understood from the corner of the eye. The unique and scandalous glory of it is the figure of a man abandoned, tortured to death to give the public an instructive thrill, and who manages to forgive, and to be loved. It is the solid assertion, in the teeth of all the evidence, that suffering matters.

Of course, there's all the business afterwards about Easter day and the empty tomb; but I don't think it's necessary to believe in that. Spring happens, even if resurrections don't. What is splendid about Christianity is that it has kept alive the memory of Good Friday, and the terrifying suspicion that it is not safe to torture anyone, even the least of your brethren. The spread of that simple idea is all the evidence of resurrection I ever found. It ought to be enough.

Andrew Brown, The *Independent*, Good Friday 1997

The Great Spirit

At a council of the Chiefs of the Six Nations, in North America, in 1805, Otetani, chief of the Senaca tribe, who had been born in 1758, gave this argument against Christian proselytising amongst his people.

Otetani was the chief spokesman for the Six Nations and through this office became a friend of George Washington. He had supported the British during the American Revolution, and was nicknamed 'Red Jacket', on account of the bright red coat the British had given him at that time.

139

Otetani eventually sought peace with the US government and he and his people supported the United States against Britain in the war of 1812.

It was the will of the Great Spirit that we should meet together this day. He orders all things and has given us a fine day for our council. He has taken his garment from before the sun and caused it to shine with brightness upon us. Our eyes are opened that we see clearly; our ears are unstopped that we have been able to hear distinctly the words you have spoken. For all these favors we thank the Great Spirit, and Him only.

Brother, this council fire was kindled by you. It was at your request that we came together at this time. We have listened with attention to what you have said. You requested us to speak our minds freely. This gives us great joy; for we now consider that we stand upright before you and can speak what we think. All have heard your voice and all speak to you now as one man. Our minds are agreed.

Brother, you say you want an answer to your talk before you leave this place. It is right you should have one, as you are a great distance from home and we do not wish to detain you. But first we will look back a little and tell you what our fathers have told us and what we have heard from the white people.

Brother, listen to what we say. There was a time when our forefathers owned this great island. Their seats extended from the rising to the setting sun. The Great Spirit had made it for the use of Indians. He had created the buffalo, the deer. And other animals for food. He had made the bear and the beaver. Their skins served us for clothing. He had scattered them over the country and taught us how to take them. He had caused the earth to produce corn for bread. All this he had done for his red children because he loved them. If we had some disputes about our hunting-ground they were generally settled without the shedding of much blood.

But an evil day came upon us. Your forefathers crossed the great water and landed on this island. Their numbers were small. They found friends and not enemies. They told us they had fled from their own country for fear of wicked men and had come here to enjoy their religion. They asked for a small seat. We took pity on them, granted their request, and they sat down among us. We gave them corn and meat; they gave us poison in return.

The white people, brother, had now found our country. Tidings were carried back and more came among us. Yet we did not fear them. We took them to be friends. They called us brothers. We believed them and gave them a larger seat. At length their numbers had greatly increased. They wanted more land; they wanted our country. Our eyes were opened and our minds became uneasy. Wars took place. Indians were hired to fight against Indians, and many of our people were destroyed. They also brought strong liquor among us. It was strong and powerful, and has slain thousands.

Brother, our seats were once large and yours were small. You have now become a great people, and we have scarcely a place left to spread our blankets. You have got our country, but are not satisfied; you want to force your religion upon us.

Brother, continue to listen. You say that you are sent to instruct us how to worship the Great Spirit agreeably to His mind; and, if we do not take hold of the religion which you white people teach we shall be unhappy hereafter. You say that you are right and we are lost. How do we know this to be true? We understand that your religion is written in a Book. If it was intended for us, as well as you, why has not the Great Spirit given to us, and not only to us, but why did He not give to our forefathers the knowledge of that Book, with the means of understanding it rightly. We only know what you tell us about it. How shall we know when to believe, being so often deceived by the white people?

Brother, you say there is but one way to worship and serve the Great Spirit. If there is but one religion, why do you white people differ so much about it? Why not all agreed, as you can all read the Book?

Brother, we do not understand these things. We are told that your religion was given to your forefathers and has been handed down from father to son. We also have a religion which was given to our forefathers and has been handed down to us, their children. We worship in that way. It teaches us to be thankful for all the favors we receive, to love each other, and to be united. We never quarrel about religion.

Brother, the Great Spirit has made us all, but He has made a difference between His white and His red children. He has given us different complexions and different customs. To you He has given the arts. To these He has not opened our eyes. We know these things to be true. Since He has made so great a difference between us in other things, why may we not conclude that He has given us a different religion according to our understanding? The Great Spirit does right. He knows what is best for His children; we are satisfied.

Brother, we do not wish to destroy your religion or take it from you. We only want to enjoy our own.

Brother, you say you have not come to get our land or our money, but to enlighten our minds. I will now tell you that I have been at your meetings and saw you collect money from the meeting. I can not tell what this money was intended for, but suppose that it was for your minister; and, if we should conform to your way of thinking, perhaps you may want some from us.

Brother, we are told that you have been preaching to the white people in this place. These people are our neighbors. We are acquainted with them. We will wait a little while and see what effect your preaching has upon them. If we find it does them good, makes them honest and less disposed to cheat Indians, we will then consider again of what you have said.

Brother, you have now heard our answer to your talk, and this is all we have to say at present. As we are going to part, we will come and take you by the hand, and hope the Great Spirit will protect you on your journey and return you safe to your friends.

Otetani, 1805

31. Homosexuality

Christian Liberation

Lesbian and gay Christians have come to see themselves in the light of the gospel and outside the homophobic attitudes by which the gospel message is stifled. From this liberation perspective, a particular emphasis may be placed on God as the creator of all things: 'Without him no created thing came into being' (*John 1.3*). From a Christian liberation perspective, a person's sexuality and so sexual orientation is a divine gift. It does not need to be renounced, concealed, pronounced sick, or regarded as deficient. Indeed, to do this is to disown what God has given.

Second, the gospel is the good news that God accepts us as we are. This was the fundamental issue of sixteenth-century controversies over what was then called justification. The sinner is made right with God neither by believing right doctrines nor by performing good works but simply on the basis of that gracious love which was sealed in Jesus Christ. The human response is to accept that we are accepted. Paul Tillich, the great Protestant theologian, often used to speak of the experience of the gospel as a voice saying to us, 'Do not seek for anything; do not perform anything; do not intend anything. *Simply accept the fact that you are accepted!*' 'If that happens to us,' he went on, 'we experience grace. Our need of divine grace is a human need, and God meets it unconditionally in Christ.'

Third, just because the acceptance of the sinner is without condition and without qualification, the trustees of the gospel message are in constant danger of reducing it to something more manageable, restricted and human. Conditionalizing strategies like, 'God loves the homosexual but hates his sin', 'God accepts the person but not the orientation', or 'Gays are accepted as long as they pretend to be straight', or 'Homosexual orientation is not sinful but homosexual acts are', etc., are all variations on a reductive theme, reducing the gospel to a merely human message and reducing homosexual people to how heterosexual people would prefer them to be. These strategies are sinful attempts to let some people off loving other people they have chosen not to like.

Fourth, a consequence of receiving the good news of God's empowering love is that one has already chosen life, 'life in all its fullness' (*John 10.10*). Sexuality is too much a part of a person's totality for it to be separated out from the rest of him or her, and repressed. It is hard to see how sexual repression and salvation are compatible:

> *For many people, in an effort to repress their sexual feelings, crush out all feeling whatsoever and live lives devoid of warmth and intimacy . . . The unloving suppression of the self's erotic needs frequently leads to the destructive acting out of those needs. What we reject in ourselves, we tend to project outward: sexism, heterosexism, homophobia, hatred of women or hatred of men, racism.*

> John McNeil, 'Taking a Chance'

God has made us to become lovers, and sin is primarily a failure to live in love. Some homosexual people, like some heterosexual people, may well have the gift of celibacy, but the majority will have a God-given desire for same-sex love, and only through the realization and expression of this love will fulfilment arrive. In all this, lesbian women and gay men are subject to the same standards of self-discipline and personal holiness as everyone else, no greater, no less.

Adrian Thatcher, *Liberating Sex*, SPCK, 1993

The Pastoral Consequences of Compulsory Celibacy

Much unhappiness among homosexuals is directly attributable to heterosexist intolerance of sexual diversity. The churches have contributed to this, and some are beginning to recognize the need for repentance and restitution. The pastoral consequences of heterosexism are apparent to all clergy. What advice is to be given to adolescents who present themselves as homosexual, or who do not identify comfortably with either classificatory term? How many could, or would, confide in their minister? How many ministers are informed about research on sexual orientation? The blanket of silence, shattered occasionally by pulpit condemnation, powerfully contributes to religious alienation and the internalization of guilt, whereas an uncompromising Christian sexual theology sees sexuality, regardless of orientation, as a gift from God, which bestows the power of self-acceptance and confers the grace of responsible, joyful loving.

Pastoral advice commonly leads to an ultimatum. Remain celibate or look for an opposite-sex partner. Since orientation is sometimes not as fixed as the labels 'homosexual' and 'lesbian' imply, the expectation of definiteness is sometimes unrealized, leading to unhappiness and confusion. But celibacy is a 'gift' (*Corinthians 7.7*), and that term implies most of us do not have it. A quarter of gay men are married (to women). Why? Possible reasons why gay men and women marry include 'insufficient awareness of one's gayness at the time of marriage', 'a conscious desire to escape from the knowledge of one's gayness', 'rational choice', and social and familial pressures.

In most cases 'the heterosexual spouse is not *aware of his or her partner's homosexuality*' (Jack Babuscio, *We Speak for Ourselves: The Experiences of Gay Men and Lesbians*, SPCK, 1988). Simple social acceptance of sexual diversity and a mature sexual theology which celebrates sexuality without regard to fixed orientations would help immeasurably. Perhaps one of the saddest pastoral situations is the Christian lesbian or gay person who, lacking the gift of *celibacy* and aching for love, confuses the influence of bad procreative theology and insistent heterosexism with the call of God to live a celibate life. Celibacy is indeed a gift; compulsory celibacy never.

Adrian Thatcher, Liberating Sex, SPCK, 1993.

32. Judgment

When we are coldly discussing a man's career, sneering at his mistakes, blaming him for his rashness, and labelling his opinions – 'Evangelical and narrow' or 'Latitudinarian and Pantheistic' or 'Anglican and supercilious' – that man, in his solitude, is perhaps shedding hot tears because his sacrifice is a hard one, because his strength and patience are failing him to speak the difficult word and do the difficult deed.

George Eliot (1819–80)

You can be certain of this: when the Day of Judgement comes. We shall not be asked what we have read, but what we have done; not how well we have spoken, but how well we have lived.

Thomas à Kempis (*c*. 1380–1471)

33. Money

Extracts From John Wesley's Sermon on 'The Use of Money'

'The love of money', we know, 'is the root of all evil'; but not the
thing itself. The fault does not lie in the money, but in them that
use it . . . It is therefore of the highest concern, that all who fear
God know how to employ this valuable talent . . . And, perhaps,
all the instructions which are necessary for this may be reduced to
three plain rules, by the exact observance whereof we may approve
ourselves faithful stewards of 'the mammon of unrighteousness'.

Rule One: Gain all you can . . . but . . .

The first of these (rules) is 'Gain all you can'. Here we speak
like the children of the world: we meet them on their own ground.
And it is bounden duty to do this: we ought to gain all we can,
without buying gold too dear, without paying more for it than it
is worth. But this it is certain we ought not to do; we ought not
to gain money at the expense of life, nor, (which effect the same
thing) at the expense of our health. Therefore, no gain whatsoever
should induce us to enter into, or to continue in, any employ,
which is of such a kind, or is attended with so hard or so long
labour, as to impair our constitution. Neither should we begin
or continue in any business which necessarily deprives us of
proper seasons for food and sleep in such a proportion as our
nature requires. Indeed, there is a great difference here. Some
employments are absolutely and totally unhealthy; as those which
imply the dealing much with arsenic, or other hurtful minerals,
or the breathing of air tainted with streams of melting lead, which

148

must at length destroy the firmest constitution.

We are, secondly, to gain all we can without hurting our mind any more than our body. For neither may we hurt this: we must preserve at all events, the spirit of a healthful mind. Therefore, we may not engage or continue in any sinful trade; any that is contrary to the law of God, or of our country. Such are all that necessarily imply our robbing or defrauding the king of his lawful customs. For it is, at least, as sinful to defraud the king of his right, as to rob our fellow subjects: and the king has full as much right to his customs as we have to our houses and apparel. Other businesses there are which, however innocent in themselves, cannot be followed with innocence now; at least not in England; such, for instance, as will not afford a competent maintenance without cheating or lying, or conformity to some custom which is not consistent with a good conscience: these, likewise, are sacredly to be avoided, whatever gain they may be attended with, provided we follow the custom of the trade; for, to gain money, we must not lose our souls.

We are, thirdly, to gain all we can, without hurting our neighbour. But this we may not, cannot do, if we love our neighbour as ourselves. We cannot, if we love every one as ourselves, hurt any one *in his substance*. We cannot devour the increase of his lands, and perhaps the lands and houses themselves, by *gaining*, by overgrown bills (whether on account of physic, or law, or anything else), or by requiring or taking such interest as even the laws of our country forbid. Hereby all pawnbroking is excluded: seeing, whatever good we might do thereby, all unprejudiced men see, with grief, to be abundantly overbalanced by the evil. And if it were otherwise, yet we are not allowed to 'do evil that good may come'. We cannot, consistent with brotherly love, sell our goods below the market price; we cannot study to ruin our neighbour's trade, in order to advance our own; much less can we entice away, or receive, any of his servants or workmen whom he has need of. None can gain by swallowing up his neighbour's substance, without gaining the damnation of hell!

Rule Two: Save All You Can

. . . Having gained all you can, by honest wisdom, and un-wearied diligence, the second rule of Christian prudence is, 'Save all you can'.

Waste no part of it in curiously adorning your houses; in super-fluous or expensive furniture; in costly pictures, painting, gilding, books; in elegant rather than useful gardens.

Lay out nothing to gratify the pride of life, to gain the admiration or praise of men. This motive of expense is frequently interwoven with one or both of the former. Men are expensive in diet, or apparel or furniture, not barely to please their appetite, or to gratify their eye, or their imagination, but their vanity too.

Who would expend anything in gratifying these desires if he considered that to gratify them is to increase them? Nothing can be more certain than this: daily experience shows the more they are indulged, they increase the more.

Rule Three: Give All You Can

. . . All this is nothing if a man go not forward, if he does not point all this at a farther end. Nor indeed, can a man properly be said to save anything if he only lays it up. You may as well throw your money into the sea as bury it in the earth. And you may as well bury it in the earth as in your chest, or in the Bank of England. Not to use, is effectually to throw it away. If, therefore, you would indeed 'make yourselves friends of the mammon of unrighteous-ness' add the third rule to the two pre-ceding. Having, first, gained all you can, and, secondly, saved all you can, then 'give all you can'.

. . . You see the nature and extent of truly Christian prudence, so far as it relates to the use of that great talent, money. Gain all you can without hurting yourself or your neighbour, in soul or body, by applying hereto with unintermitted diligence, and with all the understanding which God has given you; – save all you can, by cutting off every expense which serves only to indulge foolish desire; to gratify either the desire of the flesh, the desire of the eye, or the pride of life; waste nothing, living or dying, on sin or folly, whether for yourself or your children; – and then give all you can, or, in other words, give all you have to God.

John Wesley, 1703–91

Dear Patty,

You do not consider, money never stays with me: it would burn me if it did. I throw it out of my hands as soon as possible, lest it should find a way into my heart. Therefore you should have spoken to me while I was in London, and before Miss Lewen's money flew away. However, I know not but I may still spare you five pounds, provided you will not say, 'I will never ask you again', because that is more than you can tell; and you must not promise more than you can perform.

John Wesley,
letter to Mrs Hall, 6 October 1768

Bristol
9 September 1776

Sir,

I have two silver teaspoons at London and two at Bristol. This is all the plate which I have at present. And I shall not buy any more while so many round me want bread.
I am, Sir,
Your most humble servant,

John Wesley

Letter to the Commissioner of Excise who had demanded an immediate answer to an enquiry about the possession of silver plate on which there was a tax. The Commissioner's letter had implied that it could not be doubted that Wesley possessed plate.

Ethical Investment

The Sermon on the Mount came under scrutiny in the High Court this week. The particular phrase quoted was where Jesus said,

'Do not lay up for yourselves treasure on earth, but in heaven'.

Such advice, said a leading barrister, was feckless. Now, that's a good old adjective that's rarely used these days. It means ineffective or futile.

The barrister was speaking in a debate about investments. It was part of a friendly action brought by the Bishop of Oxford and others against the Church Commissioners. They were trying to test how far Charity law permits a body like churches to operate their investment portfolio not according to where they can get the highest returns but to where the money can do the most good, or at any rate the least harm. The Court has at the moment reserved judgement.

Anyone who has money to spare and to save has to ask the same question about how they should invest it. There's no doubt that the Bible, both in the Hebrew Scriptures and in the New Testament, is strongly opposed to the principle of making profit out of lending money to others. The medieval church insisted that money made from trade was to be used for the benefit of the community. Nowadays people who on other matters of personal morality may take a rigid Biblical line, on matters of investment are more inclined to conform to modern understanding of the way the market works and wealth is created. They may however want to apply ethical criteria to their choice of firms in which to invest their money.

Some years ago the British Council of Churches set up an Ethical Investment Research Service to help them do that. At first it concentrated on what might be called negative criteria. It advised against investing in firms with a large stake in the arms industry, in alcohol, in South Africa or in other repressive regimes. There are now several ethical investment unit trusts. Nowadays many of them follow positive criteria too. They promise to invest in businesses that are benefiting the community, and are environment-friendly. This led to a headline in a recent financial survey,

'Green issues sprout from every window in the city'.

In Biblical imagery heaven is depicted as a city – one where the rivers run with pure water, the trees grow for the healing of the nations, the gates are open to people from all over the world, and the whole community is united in the worship of God who rules in justice and peace. In advising us to lay up treasure in heaven Jesus went on to remind us that where our treasure is there will our heart be also. This doesn't seem to me to be futile advice. If our money is invested in enterprises that are attempting even modestly to realise the values of the kingdom of heaven here on earth then maybe our energies will become more directed to that end too.

Dr Pauline Webb, BBC *Thought For The Day*, 12 October 1991

34. Original Sin

The doctrine propounded by Augustine is that the guilt of Adam's first sin is inherited by the entire human race so that all humanity is born in a state of sin, and therefore in a state of condemnation and liable to eternal damnation. This is a harsh doctrine that presents us with an image of a terrible, implacable God, a concept which appears to be at odds with the image and nature of God presented by Jesus Christ. It is also a doctrine peculiar to the Western Church. It is not held by Jews, Greek Orthodox Christians or Muslims.

Original Sin and Adam

Banished from Paradise, after his sin, Adam bound his offspring also with the penalty of death and damnation, that offspring which by sinning he had corrupted in himself, as in a root; so that whatever progeny was born (through carnal concupiscence, by which a fitting retribution for his disobedience was bestowed upon him) from himself and his spouse – who was the cause of his sin and the companion of his damnation – would drag through the ages the burden of Original Sin, by which it would itself be dragged through manifold errors and sorrows, down to that final and never-ending torment with the rebel angels.

Augustine (354–430), from *Enchiridion ad Laurentium*

Original Sin and Eve

Do you know that you are each an Eve? The sentence of God on this sex of yours lives in this age: the guilt must of necessity live too. *You* are the devil's gateway; *you* are the unsealer of that forbidden tree; *you* are the first deserter of the divine law; *you* are she who persuaded him whom the devil was not valiant enough to attack. *You* so carelessly destroyed man, God's image. On account of your desert, even the Son of God had to die.

Tertullian (160–220), from 'On Female Dress'

Original Sin – Refuted

Everything good and everything evil, in respect of which we are either worthy of praise or of blame, is *done by us*, not *born in us*. We are not born in our full development, but with a capacity for good and evil; we are begotten as well without virtue as without vice, and before the activity of our own personal will there is nothing in man but what God has stored in him.

Pelagius, *c.* 400, from 'De Peccato Originali'

35. Prayers

ℊℊℊℊℊℊ

We, ignorant of ourselves,
Beg often our own harms, which the wise powers
Deny us for our good; so find we profit
by losing our prayers.

William Shakespeare (1564–1616), *Antony and Cleopatra* act 2, sc.1

My words fly up, my thoughts remain below.
Words without thoughts never to heaven go.

William Shakespeare (1564–1616), *Hamlet* act 3, sc. 3

Jesus falls, carrying his cross

Lord,
You stumble and fall
and I watch, appalled
as you multiply,
as a group of you stare at me,
large-eyed and starving.
I cannot believe what I see,
rib-taut hunger accuses me,
pot-bellied children
deep in the blank-eyed hollow of despair
Ignore me.
And there you lie,
and there,

condemned to life
in a corrugated, cardboard,
polythene prison.
You stumble and fall
at the feet of the rich
and deeply distressed,
I throw you a crumb.

Frank Topping, *An Impossible God*

Part 4 Politics, the Law and the State

36. Crime and Punishment

Myra Hindley will never be free. Michael Howard has told her this officially. It will take a brave Home Secretary to release this woman and we do not expect such bravery from Michael Howard. Why should this woman be free when the parents of the children she helped murder have had to live with a life sentence of grief? Why doesn't she do the decent thing demanded in countless tabloid editorials and commit suicide?

There is of course more than one way of taking a life and we have taken Hindley's. The average life sentence is 14 years: she has been in prison more than three decades. No one seriously believes that she will be a danger to anyone if released. She is a 54-year-old woman with osteoporosis yet we refuse to see her this way. Instead she is forever a peroxided evil tart who didn't have the grace to go mad as Brady did; a woman who defied the basic instincts of her gender. It's possible according to the certifiable Dr. Raj Persuad, a consultant psychiatrist employed by the *Daily Mail*, that upon release she could even meet another Brady. Once more she could become the accomplice of a man obsessed with Nazism and sadism. Once more she could . . .

So Hindley will die in jail and the anguished parents of her victims still raw with pain will declare this 'the best day of their lives'. The judge at her trial was reported as saying at the time that he didn't believe she was beyond redemption but politicians, not the judiciary, have decided that she is.

Her supporters, – including Lord (Loopy himself) Longford – appear to have done her more harm than good by their very unworldliness. How would you feel, the mob screams at this 91-year-old man, if it were your child? How would you feel? Wouldn't

161

you want to kill them? Destroy their life as they have destroyed yours? That's what it is to be human and by implication the likes of Lord Longford are as devoid of human response as Hindley herself.

Yet Longford, sustained by his Catholicism, is one of the few public figures who are not embarrassed to talk about forgiveness or at least its possibility. Forgiveness does not make for sexy headlines. No, all these years later we prefer headlines like, 'Evil Myra's Lesbian Love Calls Are Axed' or 'Brady: Don't Set Myra Free' or 'Rose West and Myra Hold Hands'. We prefer to leave Hindley in jail, locked forever in the terrible events of the mid-sixties.

She struggles in her letters to explain herself but never shows enough remorse or understanding of what she has done. What would enough be? She is cold, manipulative, detached, analysing herself as if she were only ever an iconic media representation, never a woman of the flesh with blood on her hands. As time goes by she becomes increasingly articulate and we understand her less and less, condemn her more and more. In 1978 it was thought that she should serve a shorter sentence than Brady. In 1990 the Home Secretary decided that she should serve a whole life sentence. Have the sentences been rejigged as her release date draws nearer and nearer or have we become less forgiving? How has this woman moved from being possibly redeemable to being utterly beyond redemption in the course of 30 years? If we do not begin to understand this then the lynch mob rules indeed.

During the trial of the boy murderers of James Bulger, young men gathered at the court. Blake Morrison in his book *As If* describes them thus: 'The men . . . had come wanting to kill the kids who had killed the kid, because there's nothing worse than killing a kid.' Morrison's troubled and troubling book attempts to understand what happened at that trial, how children were put on trial as if they were adults by adults who should have but didn't let themselves know better.

By the anniversary of James's death those sad, fat little 10-year-olds had already joined the pantheon of 'Britain's most reviled killers'. The spectacle was raised that they may be freed in their early twenties and already a campaign has been mounted to keep them in prison forever. Various Bulger relatives had vowed to kill the two on release, just as the relatives of Hindley's victims promise to murder her.

Surely if we have any faith in rehabilitation which after all is still one of the professed aims of incarceration, then children have more chance of being rehabilitated than adults, yet if we continue to judge these boys as adult murderers then no forgiveness is possible.

It is difficult to talk about forgiveness from a secular viewpoint, we don't have enough markers. We are merely proclaiming our faith in an idea. We sound far too wishy-washy, far too liberal. Yet as Morrison writes, 'Only a culture without hope cannot forgive – a culture that doesn't believe in progress or redemption. Have we so little faith in ourselves we can't accept the possibility of maturation, change, cure?'

The answer is that we have little faith indeed. While the language of therapy crops up everywhere – the concepts of repression, denial and projection are commonplace – our belief in actual change is small. Tinkering with one's psyche may be positive but the chance of deep and meaningful change we feel remains remote. So we sit in judgement, closing down on people whose worlds closed down long ago.

I fear it is already too late for Hindley. Her case has already been taken out of the hands of the judiciary and become obscenely tied to political posturing that does nothing constructive for any one, least of all the red-eyed parents of her victims who must relive their trauma time and again for the rest of us. Hindley is right to argue that she has now become a political prisoner. But it is not too late for Bulger's killers, and to bracket them alongside her and Brady is another kind of crime altogether. If our justice system is to be based on the feelings of the bereaved alone then we may as well hang every killer and be done with it.

It is unfashionable in these days of law and order to insist that prison must serve some purpose beyond that of simply punishment, but we must. Does to align oneself with loony peers, judges and other professionals who support Hindley's release mean that one has been duped by a scheming middle-aged woman? Is it too much to ask for a penal system that is no longer fuelled by the lust for revenge alone?

We have a choice as to whether we are ruled by our baser instincts or whether we believe it is possible to rise above them. In our hearts we may never accept that those individuals who have taken the lives of children are ever able to do this. Collectively, however, we must have faith in that possibility, for without it all sentences become death sentences.

Forgiveness does not mean forgetting or excusing hideous crimes, it means only that we believe in the potential for change, that we choose life over death, that faced with horrific acts and evil monsters, we endeavour in whatever way we can to remain human. If this is asking so much then let each and every one of us stand in the enormous queue of those who are prepared to do to Hindley what she did to others, to join the lynch mob. Then we might know what she knows and we might know what it is like to be no longer human.

Suzanne Moore, The *Independent*, 7 February 1997

37. 'Corruptible to Incorruptible'

❧❧❧❧❧❧❧❧❧❧❧❧

The last words of King Charles I. Charles was executed on 30 January 1649, at the Banqueting House in Whitehall, having been found guilty of waging war against his own people. In an attempt to make his 'public' execution as private as possible the scaffold had been built low and at a considerable distance from the public, who, as a result, were not able to hear his speech. He could therefore address only those in the group that stood immediately around him. He linked his prayers with St Stephen, the first martyr, and described himself as a martyr of the people, and is still remembered as Charles the Martyr whether or not he was guilty of the charges against him.

I shall be very little heard of anybody here; I shall therefore speak a word unto you here; indeed I could hold my peace very well, if I did not think that holding my peace would make some men think that I did submit to the guilt, as well as to the punishment; but I think it is my duty to God first and then to my country for to clear myself both as an honest man and a good king and a good Christian. I shall begin first with my innocency. In troth I think it not very needful for me to insist long upon this, for all the world knows that I never did begin a war with the two Houses of Parliament, and I call God to witness, to whom I must shortly make my account, that I never did intend for to encroach upon their privileges; they began upon me, it is the militia, they began upon, they contest that the militia was mine, but they thought it fit for to have it from me; and to be short, if anybody will look to the dates of the commissions, of their commissions and mine, and likewise to the declarations, will see clearly that they began these unhappy troubles, not I, so that as the guilt of these enormous crimes that are laid against me, I hope in God that God will clear me of it, I will not, I am in charity; God forbid that I should lay it upon the two Houses of Parliament; there is no necessity of either, I hope they are free of this guilt, for I do believe that ill instruments between them and me has been the chief cause of all this bloodshed; so that by way of speaking as I find myself clear of this, I hope (and pray God) that they may too: yet for all this, God forbid that I should be so ill a Christian as not to say that God's judgements are just upon me: many times he does pay justice by an unjust sentence, that is ordinary; I will only say this, that an unjust sentence that I suffered for to take effect is punished now, by an unjust sentence upon me; that is, so far I have said, to show you that I am an innocent man.

Now for to show you that I am a good Christian: I hope there is a good man that will bear me witness, that I have forgiven all the world; even those in particular that have been the chief causes of my death; who they are, God knows, I do not desire to know, I pray God forgive them. But this is not all; my charity must go farther, I wish that they may repent, for indeed they have committed a great sin in that particular; I pray God with Saint Stephen that they may take the right way to the peace of the kingdom, for my charity commands me not only to forgive particular men, but my charity commands me to endeavour to the last gasp the peace of the kingdom: so, sirs, I do with all my soul, and I do hope (there is some here will carry it further) that they may endeavour the peace of the kingdom. Now, sirs, I must show you both how you are out of the way and will put you in a way; first, you are out of the way, for certainly all the way you ever had yet as I could find by anything is in the way of conquest; certainly this is an ill way, for conquest, sir, in my opinion is never just, except there be a good just cause, either for the matter of wrong or just title, and then if you go beyond it, the first quarrel that you have to it, that makes it unjust at the end, that was just at first: But if it be only matter of conquest, then it is a great robbery; as a pirate said to Alexander, that he was the great robber, he was but a petty robber, and so, sir, I do think the way that you are in, is much out of the way.

Now, sir, for to put you in the way, believe it you will never do right, nor God will never prosper you, until you give God his due, the King his due (that is, my successor), and the people their due; I am as much for them as any of you: you must give God his due by regulating rightly his church according to his Scripture which is now out of order: for to set you in a way particularly now I cannot, but only this, a national synod freely called, freely debating among themselves, must settle this, when that every opinion is freely and clearly heard.

For the king, indeed I will not . . . [Charles then observed a gentleman touching the axe, and said to him, 'hurt not the axe that may hurt me.'] For the King: the laws of the land will clearly instruct you for that; therefore, because it concerns my own particular, I only give you a touch of it.

For the people. And truly I desire their liberty and freedom, as much as anybody whomsoever; but I must tell you that their liberty and their freedom consists in having of government those laws by which their life and their goods may be most their own. It is not for having share in government, sir, that is nothing pertaining to them. A subject and a sovereign are clean different things; and therefore, unto they do that, I mean, that you do put the people in that liberty as I say, certainly they will never enjoy themselves.

Sirs, it was for this that now I am come here: if I would have given way to an arbitrary way, for to have all laws changed according to the power of the sword, I needed not to have come here; and therefore, I tell you (and I pray God it be not laid to your charge) that I am the martyr of the people.

In troth, sirs, I shall not hold you much longer; for I will only say this to you, that in truth I could have desired some little time longer, because that I would have put this I have said in a little more order, and a little better digested, than I have done; and therefore I hope you will excuse me.

I have delivered my conscience, I pray God, that you do take those courses that are best for the kingdom, and your own salvation.

[Dr Juxon speaks, 'Will Your Majesty, though it may be very well known, Your Majesty's affections to religion, yet it may be expected that you should say somewhat to the world's satisfaction.']

I thank you very heartily, my lord, for that; I had almost forgotten it. In troth, sirs, my conscience in religion, I think, is very well known to the world; and therefore I declare before you all that I die a Christian according to the profession of the church of England, as I found it left me by my father; and this honest man [pointing to Dr Juxon] will witness it. Sirs, excuse me for this same. I have a good cause, and I have a gracious God; I will say no more. I go from a corruptible to an incorruptible crown, where no disturbance can be, no disturbance in the world.

King Charles I, 30 January 1649

38. Colonies

Africa

When white men first came, they had the Bible, and we had the land. Now, we have the Bible and they have our land.

Archbishop Desmond Tutu

India

It is terrible to see our middle-class journals and speakers calling for the destruction of Delhi, and the indiscriminate massacre of prisoners . . .

To read the letters of our officers at the commencement of the outbreak it seemed as if every subaltern had the power to hang or shoot as many natives as he pleased, and they spoke of the work of blood with as much levity as if they were hunting wild animals . . . It will be a happy day when England has not an acre of territory in Continental Asia. But . . . where do we find even an individual who is not imbued with the notion that England would sink to ruin if she were deprived of her Indian Empire? Leave me, then, to my pigs and sheep, which are not labouring under any such delusions.

Extracts from a letter to John Bright from Richard Cobden,
22 September 1857

Mahatma Gandhi and Non-violent Protest

This statement was made by Gandhi at his trial for sedition in three articles he had written for his magazine Young India. *Gandhi had already pleaded guilty.*

Non-violence is the first article of my faith. It is the last article of my faith. I had either to submit to a system which I considered has done an irreparable harm to my country or incur the risk of the mad fury of my people bursting forth when they understood the truth from my lips. I know that my people have sometimes gone mad. I am deeply sorry for it; and I am therefore, here, to submit not to a light penalty but to the highest penalty. I do not ask for mercy. I do not plead any extenuating act. I am here, therefore, to invite and submit to the highest penalty that can be inflicted on me for what in law is a deliberate crime and what appears to me to be the highest duty of a citizen. The only course open to you, Mr. Judge, is as I am going to say in my statement, either you resign your post or inflict on me the severest penalty if you believe that the system and law you are assisting to administer are good for the people. I do not expect that kind of conversion. But by the time I have finished with my statement you will, perhaps, have a glimpse of what is raging within my breast to run this maddest risk which a sane man can run.

Little do town-dwellers know how the semi-starved masses of Indians are slowly sinking into lifelessness. Little do they know that their miserable comfort represents the brokerage they get for the work they do for the foreign exploiter, that the profit and the brokerage are sucked from the masses. Little do they realize that the government established by law in British India is carried on for this exploitation of the masses. No sophistry, no jugglery in figures can explain away the evidence in skeletons in many villages present to the naked eye. I have no doubt whatsoever that both England and the town-dwellers of India will have the answer, if there is a God above, for this crime against humanity which is perhaps unequalled in history. The law itself in this country has been used to serve the foreign exploiter. My experience of political cases in India leads me to the conclusion that in nine out of every ten the condemned men were innocent. Their crime consisted in love of their country. In ninety-nine cases out of a hundred, justice has been denied to Indians as against Europeans in the courts of India. This is not an exaggerated picture. It is the experience of almost every Indian who has had anything to do with such cases. In my opinion the administration of the law is thus prostituted consciously or unconsciously for the benefit of the exploiter.

The greatest misfortune is that Englishmen and their Indian associates in the administration of the country do not know that they are engaged in the crime I have attempted to describe. I am satisfied that many English and Indian officials honestly believe that they are administering one of the best systems devised in the world and that India is making steady though slow progress. They do not know that a subtle but effective system of terrorism and an organized display of force on the one hand and the deprivation of all powers of retaliation or self defense on the other have emasculated the people and induced in them the habit of simulation. This awful habit has added to the ignorance and the self-deception of the administrators. Section 124-A under which I am happily charged is perhaps the prince among the political sections of the Indian Penal Code designed to suppress the liberty of the citizen. Affection cannot be manufactured or regulated by law. If one has no affection for a person or a thing one should be free to give the fullest expression to his dissatisfaction so long as he does not contemplate, promote or incite to violence. But the section under which Mr Banner and I are charged is one under which mere promotion of disaffection is a crime. I have studied some of the cases tried under it, and I know that some of the most loved of India's patriots have been convicted under it. I consider it a privilege, therefore, to be charged under it. I have endeavoured to give in their briefest outline the reasons for my disaffection. I have no personal ill-will against any single administrator much less can I have any disaffection towards the king's person. But I hold it a virtue to be disaffected towards a government which in its totality has done more harm to India than any previous system. India is less manly under the British rule than she ever was before. Holding such a belief, I consider it to be a sin to have affection for the system. And it has been a precious privilege for me to be able to write what I have in the various articles tendered in evidence against me.

In fact I believe that I have rendered a service to India and England by showing in non-co-operation the way out of the unnatural state in which both are living. In my humble opinion, non-co-operation with evil is as much a duty as is co-operating with good. But in the past, non-co-operation has been deliberately expressed in violence to the evildoer. I am endeavouring to show to my countrymen that violent non-co-operation only multiplies evil and that as evil can only be sustained by violence, withdrawal of support of evil requires complete abstention from violence. Non-violence implies voluntary submission to the penalty for non-co-operation with evil. I am here, therefore, to invite and submit cheerfully to the highest penalty that can be inflicted upon me for what in law is deliberate crime and what appears to me to be the highest duty of a citizen. The only course open to you, the Judge and the Assessors, is to resign your posts and thus disassociate yourselves from evil if you feel that the law you are called upon to administer is an evil and that in reality I am innocent, or to inflict on me the severest penalty if you believe that the system and the law you are assisting to administer are good for the people of this country and that my activity is therefore injurious to the public weal.

After this statement, Gandhi was sentenced to six years' imprisonment. Gandhi thanked the judge for his courtesy. He was imprisoned again twice in the thirties and once in the forties. He later worked with the British authorities to achieve independence for India, which was eventually declared twenty-five years later. Sadly he was assassinated in 1948.

39. Democracy

❧❧❧ ❧❧❧ ❧❧❧ ❧❧❧ ❧❧❧ ❧❧❧

'Government of the people, by the people, for the people'

Abraham Lincoln's Gettysburg address was intended to be a Presidential footnote, a mere formality at the dedication of the cemetery for soldiers who fell at the Battle of Gettysburg. The main address of the occasion was given by Edward Everett who was the most celebrated American orator of his day. Everett had been Governor of Massachusetts four times; he had been a senator, Secretary of State, President of Harvard and Ambassador to Great Britain. His 'oration' had lasted for over two hours before Lincoln spoke.

Lincoln's speech consisted of less than three hundred words which he delivered in less than three minutes. Everett's 'eloquence' has been forgotten, Lincoln's 'plain' language, which somehow encapsulated America's hopes and dreams, and the aspirations of the American constitution, has gone into history as one of the greatest and most frequently quoted speeches of all time.

Fellow-countrymen – Four score and seven years ago our fathers brought forth on this continent a new nation, conceived in Liberty, and dedicated to the proposition that all men are created equal.

Now we are engaged in a great civil war, testing whether that nation, or any nation so conceived and so dedicated, can long endure. We are met on a great battlefield of that war. We have come to dedicate a portion of that held, as a final resting-place for those who here gave their lives that that nation might live. It is altogether fit and proper that we should do this.

But, in a larger sense, we cannot dedicate – we cannot consecrate – we cannot hallow this ground. The brave men, living and dead, who struggled here, have consecrated it, far above our poor power to add or detract. The world will little note, nor long remember, what we say here, but it can never forget what they did here. It is for us, the living, rather, to be dedicated here to the unfinished work which they who fought here have thus far so nobly advanced. It is rather for us to be here dedicated to the great task remaining before us that from these honoured dead we take increased devotion to that cause for which they gave the last full measure of devotion – that we here highly resolve that these dead shall not have died in vain – that this nation, under God, shall have a new birth of freedom and that government of the people, by the people, for the people, shall not perish from the earth.

Abraham Lincoln, Gettysburg, 19 November 1863

40. Education

'Now, what I want is, Facts. Teach these boys and girls nothing but Facts. Facts alone are wanted in life. Plant nothing else, and root out everything else. You can only form the minds of reasoning animals upon Facts: nothing else will ever be of any service to them. This is the principle on which I bring up my own children, and this is the principle on which I bring up these children. Stick to Facts, sir!'

... 'Girl number twenty,' said Mr. Gradgrind, squarely pointing with his square forefinger ... 'Give me your definition of a horse.'

(Sissy Jupe thrown into the greatest alarm by this demand.)

'Girl number twenty unable to define a horse.' Said Mr. Gradgrind for the general behoof of all the little pitchers. 'Girl number twenty possessed of no facts, in reference to one of the commonest of animals! Some boy's definition of a horse. Bitzer, yours.'

The square finger, moving here and there, lighted suddenly on Bitzer, perhaps because he chanced to sit in the same ray of sunlight which, darting in at one of the bare windows of the intensely whitewashed room, irradiated Sissy.

... 'Bitzer,' said Thomas Gradgrind. 'Your definition of a horse.'

'Quadruped. Graminivorous. Forty teeth, namely twenty-four grinders, four eye-teeth, and twelve incisive. Sheds coat in the spring; in marshy countries, sheds hoofs, too. Hoofs hard, but requiring to be shod with iron. Age known by marks in mouth.'

Thus (and much more) Bitzer.

'Now girl number twenty,' said Mr Gradgrind. 'You know what a horse is.'

She curtseyed again, and would have blushed deeper, if she could have blushed deeper than she had blushed all this time.

. . . The third gentleman now stepped forth. A mighty Man at cutting and drying, he was; a government officer; in his way (and in most other people's too), a professed pugilist; always in training, always with a system to force down the general throat like a bolus, always to be heard of at the bar of his little Public-office, ready to fight all England. To continue in fistic phraseology, he had a genius for coming up to the scratch, wherever and whatever it was, and proving himself an ugly customer. He would go in and damage any subject whatever with his right, follow up with his left, stop, exchange, counter, bore his opponent (he always fought all England) to the ropes, and fall upon him neatly. He was certain to knock the wind out of commonsense, and render that unlucky adversary deaf to the call of time. And he had it in charge from high authority to bring about the great Public-office Millennium, when Commissioners should reign upon earth.

'Very well,' said this gentleman, briskly smiling, and folding his arms. 'That's a horse. Now let me ask you girls and boys, would you paper a room with representations of horses?'

After a pause, one half of the children cried in chorus, 'Yes, sir!' Upon which the other half, seeing in the gentleman's face that Yes was wrong, cried out in chorus, 'No, sir!' – as the custom is, in these examinations.

'Of course, No. Why wouldn't you?' A pause. One corpulent slow boy, with a wheezy manner of breathing ventured the answer. Because he wouldn't paper a room at all, but would paint it. 'You must paper it,' said Thomas Gradgrind, 'whether you like it or not. Don't tell *us* you wouldn't paper it. What do you mean, boy?'

'I'll explain it to you, then.' Said the gentleman, after another and a dismal pause, 'why you wouldn't paper a room with representations of horses? Do you ever see horses walking up and down the sides of rooms in reality – in fact?'

'Yes, Sir!' from one half. 'No sir!' from the other.

'Of course no,' said the gentleman, with an indignant look at the wrong half.

'Why, then, you are not to see anywhere, what you don't see in fact; you are not to have anywhere, what you don't have in fact.

What is called Taste, is only another name for fact.'

Thomas Gradgrind nodded his approbation.

'This is a new principle, a discovery, a great discovery,' said the gentleman. 'Now I'll try you again. Suppose you were going to carpet a room. Would you use a carpet having a representation of flowers upon it?'

There being a general conviction by this time that 'No, Sir!' was always the right answer to this gentleman, the chorus of No was very strong. Only a few feeble stragglers said Yes; among them Sissy Jupe.

'Girl number twenty,' said the gentleman, smiling in the calm strength of knowledge. Sissy blushed, and stood up.

'So you would carpet your room – or your husband's room, if you were a grown woman, and had a husband – with representations of flowers would you,' said the gentleman. 'Why would you?'

'If you please, sir, I am very fond of flowers,' returned the girl.

'And is that why you would put tables and chairs upon them, and have people walking over them with heavy boots?'

'It wouldn't hurt them, sir. They wouldn't crush and wither if you please, sir. They would be the pictures of what was very pretty and pleasant, and I would fancy – '

'Ay, ay, ay! But you mustn't fancy,' cried the gentleman, quite elated by coming so happily to his point. 'That's it! You are never to fancy.'

'You are not, Cecilia Jupe,' – Thomas Gradgrind solemnly repeated, 'to do anything of that kind.'

'Fact, fact, fact!' said the gentleman. And 'Fact, fact, fact!' repeated Thomas Gradgrind.

'You are to be in all things regulated and governed,' said the gentleman, 'by fact. We hope to have, before long, a board of fact, composed of commissioners of fact, who will force the people to be a people of fact, and of nothing but fact. You must discard the word Fancy altogether. You have nothing to do with it. You are not to have, in any object of use or ornament, what would be a contradiction in fact. You don't walk upon flowers in fact; you cannot be allowed to walk upon flowers in carpets. You don't find that foreign birds and butterflies come and perch upon your crockery. You never meet with quadrupeds going up and down walls; you must not have quadrupeds represented upon walls. You must use,' said the gentleman, 'for all these purposes, Combinations and modifications (in primary colours) of mathematical figures which are susceptible of proof and demonstration. This is the new discovery. This is fact. This is taste.'

The girl curtseyed, and sat down. She was very young, and she looked as if she were frightened by the matter of fact prospect the world afforded.

Charles Dickens, *Hard Times*

41. Ownership

A case of heartless robbery was exposed the other day when the Duke of Hamilton, a local coalmaster named Frederick Michael Thomas Andrew Sucker, and several others were charged with having conspired together to rob an old miner named Dick M'Gonnagle. Great interest was manifested in the case, the Court being densely crowded. The Magistrate, in opening the proceedings, said that owing to the very grave nature of the charge, and the immense interest to the community, he had decided to adopt the French mode of procedure and would commence by asking the prisoners to submit themselves to examination. The Coalmaster then entered the witness box to be examined by the Magistrate.

Magistrate: What is your name?
Prisoner: Frederick Michael Thomas Andrew Sucker, Sir.
Magistrate: You have a great many names.
Prisoner: I protest, Sir.
Magistrate: I did not ask you your occupation. I desire to know how you came to be possessed of so many names?
Prisoner: I can't answer your question, Sir.
Magistrate: Ah! That sounds suspicious. Now will you kindly tell us how much wealth you possess?
Prisoner: (*proudly*) One million pounds, Sir.
Magistrate: You must be an extremely able man. How did you come to have a million pounds?
Prisoner: I made it, sir.
Magistrate: Ah! do you plead guilty to manufacturing coin?

Prisoner:	(*indignantly*) No, Sir.
Magistrate:	Then will you please tell us what you mean by saying you *made* it?
Prisoner:	I earned it in business, Sir.
Magistrate:	How long have you been in business?
Prisoner:	Twenty years, Sir.
Magistrate:	You must be a very capable worker to have earned such a huge sum in such a short time?
Prisoner:	(*indignantly*) I don't work, Sir.
Magistrate:	Ah! this is interesting. You don't work and yet you have told us that in twenty years you have earned one million pounds?
Prisoner:	I own a colliery, Sir.
Magistrate:	What is a colliery?
Prisoner:	A shaft sunk perhaps a hundred fathoms in the earth also various buildings and machinery for the production of coal.
Magistrate:	Did you sink the shaft?
Prisoner:	No, Sir. I got men to do it.
Magistrate:	Did you manufacture the machinery and erect the buildings?
Prisoner:	No, Sir I am not a workman. I got others to work.
Magistrate:	This is an extraordinary case. You say other men erected the buildings, and manufactured the machinery, and sunk the shaft and yet you own the colliery? Have the workmen no share in it?
Prisoner:	No, sir. I am the sole owner.
Magistrate:	I confess I can't understand. Do you mean to tell me that those men put a colliery in full working order, and then handed it over to you without retaining even a share of it for themselves?
Prisoner:	Certainly, Sir.
Magistrate:	They must have been very rich and generous, or very foolish! Were they rich men?
Prisoner:	Oh no, Sir.
Magistrate:	Had they many collieries?
Prisoner:	Oh, none at all, Sir. They were merely workmen.
Magistrate:	What do you mean by merely workmen?

Prisoner: Merely people who work for others.

Magistrate: Surely they must be generous people. Don't they require collieries themselves?

Prisoner: They do, Sir.

Magistrate: And they own no collieries?

Prisoner: No, Sir, but I allow them to work in mine.

Magistrate: That is very kind of you, but of course not nearly so kind as their act in giving the colliery to you. Do you find you don't require the whole colliery yourself, that you can allow others also to use it?

Prisoner: Oh, you don't understand Sir. I don't work in my colliery. I allow the workmen to do so.

Magistrate: Oh, I see. After those men handed over the colliery to you, you found you had no use for it, and so returned it to save them erecting another?

Prisoner: Oh no, no, Sir. The colliery is still mine, but they work in it.

Magistrate: Really, this is very confusing. You own a Pit which you did not sink, and plant which you did not manufacture nor erect. You do not work in this colliery because you do not want to work. Those who do want to work own no colliery, and yet gave one to you. Did you beg of them to come and work in your colliery, as you had no use for it?

Prisoner: Oh, not at all, Sir. They begged me to allow them to work.

Magistrate: But why beg leave to use your colliery? Why not make one for themselves, as they had done for you?

Prisoner: I beg pardon Sir, but they could only do that by electing their own men to the County Councils and Parliament, and getting those bodies to do it, and that would never do. That would be Socialism.

Magistrate: Seems to me it would be ordinary common sense.

John Wheatley, *How the Miners Are Robbed*, 1907

181

42. Parliament

'Go, Get You Out! . . . In The Name of God, Go!'

Oliver Cromwell's dismissal of the 'Rump' Parliament in 1653.

  Cromwell wanted a new constitution. The 'Rump' Parliament had sat since the execution of Charles I in 1649. On 19 April 1653, the Rumpers had agreed to dissolve themselves. On 20 April Cromwell was informed that they were in the process of pushing through an Act to further prolong their stay in the House. Cromwell summoned a file of musketeers and hurried to the House of Commons. He left some musketeers at the door and others in the lobby, and then took his seat. At first he sat in his seat, in silence. Then, angered by what was being said, he began to speak. He put on his hat and walked up and down in the middle of the House, stamping and kicking as his anger increased. Finally when Sir Peter Wentworth accused him of immoderate language, 'unusual within the walls of Parliament', what remained of Cromwell's patience evaporated and the dam of his anger burst.

It is high time for me to put an end to your sitting in this place, which you have dishonoured by your contempt of all virtue, and defiled by your practice of every vice; ye are a factious crew, and enemies to all good government; ye are a pack of mercenary wretches, and would like Esau sell your country for a mess of pottage, and like Judas betray your God for a few pieces of money. Is there a single virtue now remaining amongst you? Is there one vice you do not possess? Ye have no more religion than my horse. Gold is your God; which of you have not barter'd your conscience for bribes? Is there a man amongst you that has the least care for the good of the Commonwealth? Ye sordid prostitutes have you not defiled this sacred place, and turn'd the Lord's temple into a den of thieves, by your immoral principles and wicked practices? Ye are grown intolerably odious to the whole nation. You who were deputed here by the people to get grievances redress'd, are yourselves become the greatest grievance. Your country therefore calls upon me to cleanse this Augean stable, by putting a final period to your iniquitous proceedings in this House; and which by God's help, and the strength he has given me, I am now come to do.

I command ye therefore, upon the peril of your lives, to depart immediately out of this place. Go, get you out! make haste! Ye venal slaves be gone!

So! Take away that shining bauble there, and lock up the doors. In the name of God, go!

Oliver Cromwell, 20 April 1653

(*The 'bauble' Cromwell referred to was the parliamentary mace which he gave to a musketeer whilst he personally ejected the Speaker of the House.*)

43. Power

Power tends to corrupt and absolute power corrupts absolutely.

Lord Acton (1834–1902)

44. Questioning State 'Truths'

Socrates, the Greek philosopher, who never wrote anything but taught by dialogue, and whose teachings were recorded by his pupil, Plato, was considered disruptive largely because he taught that everything was to be questioned, nothing taken for granted, questioning and cross-examining accepted truths, in dialogue, as he did when teaching. He believed that a good person would never knowingly do wrong, and that good people devoted themselves to virtue and truth, first and foremost, rather than the acquisition of wealth and possessions. At the age of seventy he was accused by an enemy, (or at least someone made very uncomfortable by his teachings) of 'impiety' and of 'corrupting the young'. He was found guilty and sentenced to death by drinking hemlock. At his trial Socrates made this speech in his defence.

You do wrong to think that a man of any use at all is to weigh the risk of life or death, and not consider one thing only, whether when he acts he does the right thing or the wrong, or performs the deeds of a good man or a bad.

If I should be found to be wiser than the multitude, it would be in this, that having no adequate knowledge of the Beyond, I do not presume that I have it. But one thing I do know, is that to do injustice, or turn my back on the better, is alike an evil and a disgrace. And I shall never fear a possible good, in order to avoid a certain evil. If you say to me, 'Socrates, Anytus fails to convince us. We let you go on condition that you no longer spend your life in this search, and that you give up philosophy, but if you are caught at it again you must die' – my reply is, 'Men of Athens, I honour and love you, but I shall obey God rather than you, and while I breathe, and have the strength, I shall never turn from philosophy, nor from warning and admonishing any of you I come across, not to disgrace your citizenship of a great city, renowned for its wisdom and strength, by giving your thought to reaping the largest possible harvest of wealth and honour and glory, and giving neither thought nor care that you may reach the best in judgement, truth, and the soul.'

So God bids, and I consider that never has a greater good been done you, than through my ministry in the City. For it is my one business to go about to persuade young and old alike not to make their bodies and their riches their first and engrossing care, but rather the perfecting of their souls.

Virtue does not spring from possessions, but from virtue possessions spring, and all other human blessings, whether for the individual or for society.

If that is to corrupt the youth, then it is mischievous. But that, and nothing else, is my offence, and he lies who says otherwise. Further, I would say, 'O Athenians, you can believe Anytus, or not, you may acquit, or not, but I shall not alter my conduct, no, not if I have to die a score of deaths.'

[There was an outbreak of shouting in the court when Socrates made this last point, and Socrates had to appeal to be heard. He then continued.]

You can assure yourselves of this, that being what I say, if you put me to death, you will be doing a greater injury to yourselves than to me. To do me wrong is beyond the power of a Meletus or an Anytus. Heaven does not permit the better man to be wronged by the worse. Death, exile, disgrace – Anytus and the average man may count these great evils, not I. A far greater evil is to do as he is now doing, attempting to do away with a fellow-being unjustly.

Athenians, I am far from pleading, as one might expect, for myself; it is for you I plead, lest by condemning me you should err as concerning the gift of God given to you. If you put me to death you will not easily find another of my sort, who, to use a metaphor that may cause some laughter, is attached to the state by God, as a kind of gadfly to a big generous horse, rather slow because of its very bigness and in need of being wakened up. As such, and to that end, God has attached me to the city, and all day long and everywhere I fasten on you, rousing and persuading and admonishing.

Do not be angry with me speaking the truth, for no man will escape alive who honourably and sincerely opposes you, or any other mob, and takes his stand before the many unjust and unrighteous things that would otherwise happen in the city. The man who fights for justice and right, and wishes to remain untouched, even if he expects but a short career, must occupy a private and not a public station.

Clearly, if I tried to persuade you and overcome you by entreaty, when you have taken the oath of judge, I should be teaching you not to believe that there are gods, and my very defence would be a conviction that I do not pay them regard. But that is far from being so. I believe in them as no one of my accusers believes. To you and to God I commit my cause, to judge me as seems best for me and for you.

[The court finds Socrates 'Guilty'. Socrates stands and speaks again.]

Men of Athens, many things keep me from being grieved that you have convicted me. What has happened was not unexpected by me. I am rather surprised at the number of votes on either side. I did not think the majority would be so little. As it is, the transference of thirty votes would have acquitted me.

A fine life it would be for one at my age always being driven out from one city and changing to another. For I know that wherever I go the young men will listen to my words, just as they do here. If I drive them away, they themselves will have me cast out, and if I don't drive them away their fathers and relatives will cast me out for their sakes.

[The penalty of death was then announced, to which Socrates replied:]

O Men, it is not hard to avoid death, it is far harder to avoid wrongdoing. It runs faster than death. I being slow and stricken in years am caught by the slower, but my accusers, sharp and clever as they are, by the swifter wickedness. And now I go to pay the debt of death at your hands, but they to pay the debt of crime and unrighteousness at the hand of Truth. I for my part shall abide by the award; let them see to it also. Perhaps, somehow, these things were meant to be, and I think it is well.

Wherefore, O Judges, be of good cheer about death, and know of a certainty that no evil can happen to a good man, either in life or after death. He and his are not neglected by the gods, nor has my own approaching end happened by mere chance. But I see clearly that to die and be released is better for me; and therefore the oracle gave no sign. For which reason, also, I am not angry with those who condemn me, or with my accusers; they have done me no harm, although they did not mean to do me any good; and for this I may gently blame them.

Still I have a favour to ask of them. When my sons are grown up, I would ask you, my friends, to punish them, and I would have you trouble them, as I have troubled you, if they seem to care about riches, or anything, more than about virtue; or if they pretend to be something when they are really nothing, then reprove them, as I have reproved you, for not caring about that for which they ought to care, and thinking that they are something when they are really nothing. And if you do this, I and my sons will have received justice at your hands.

The hour of departure has arrived, and we go our ways – I to die, and you to live. Which is better, God only knows.

Socrates (469–399 BC)

Index of Authors and Sources